WHAT
A CHRISTIAN
BELIEVES

WHAT
A CHRISTIAN
BELIEVES

RAY
PRITCHARD

CROSSWAY BOOKS • WHEATON, ILLINOIS
A DIVISION OF GOOD NEWS PUBLISHERS

First printing, 1998

Printed in the United States of America

ISBN 1-58134-016-8

Library of Congress Cataloging-in-Publication Data
Pritchard, Ray, 1952-
    What a Christian believes / Ray Pritchard.
        p.   cm.
    Includes bibliographical references.
    ISBN 1-58134-016-8
    1. Theology, Doctrinal—Popular works.   I. Title.
BT77.P75   1998
230—dc21   98-23783

11	10	09	08	07	06	05	04	03	02	01	00	99	98
15	14	13	12	11	10	9	8	7	6	5	4	3	2	1

*This book is dedicated to the three congregations
it has been my privilege to serve as pastor:*

*Redeemer Covenant Church, Downey, California
Northeast Bible Church, Garland, Texas
Calvary Memorial Church, Oak Park, Illinois*

CONTENTS

ACKNOWLEDGMENTS

Many years ago I first learned the Gospel from Rev. Ed McCollum, to whom I owe a great debt.

I am grateful also to Mr. And Mrs. Ira Schnell, Dr. J. O. Colley, Alvin and Ruth Johnson, Rev. Dudley Lynch, Mrs. R. C. Thomas, Mr. and Mrs. Hal Kirby, Sr., Neil Nation, and Marshall Crawley. Each person has played a vital role in my spiritual journey.

In my formative years I cut my teeth spiritually with a group of rambunctious teenagers who later became strong men of God: Rick Suddith, Phil Newton, Neil Jones, Jeff Hargett, David Neal, Jeff McAllister, Ricky Kirkpatrick, Paul Lynch, Joey Newton, Ken Sibley, Butch Henderson, Bruce Thorn, and Ken Aycock. Special thanks to my brother Alan who came to Christ exactly one week after I did.

Andy McQuitty, pastor of Irving Bible Church, Irving, Texas, gave me the idea for the sermon series upon which this book is based. Brian Bill, missionary with Project Aztec in Mexico City, offered key insights to several chapters of this book. My debt can be seen in the footnotes and even more in the affection I feel for both of them.

Brian Ondracek and Ted Griffin of Crossway Books waited patiently while I finished this manuscript.

Finally, I am grateful to my wife, Marlene, and our three boys—Josh, Mark, and Nick—for their love and constant encouragement.

INTRODUCTION

Every statement of faith is in the end a personal statement. I cannot speak for you, nor you for me, which is why the Apostles' Creed begins with the words "I believe." Questions of faith are always singular because no one else can believe for you—even though some people would like to. I also know skeptics who would gladly believe if only they could find a way to borrow some faith. And I know Christians who struggle mightily to believe the hymns they sing on Sunday morning.

This short book is my own personal statement of faith. It doesn't include everything I believe, but it does touch on the central truths that Christians hold in common. Recently while surfing the Internet I happened to find a huge site called "The Atheism Web." The home page contained a well-written essay called "An Introduction to Atheism." After answering many questions (most of them from Christians), the writer concluded with ten fundamental ideas that most atheists promote. The last and most important one reads simply: "All beliefs should be open to question."

I happen to believe he is exactly right. Even though I am profoundly convinced that Christianity is true and that Jesus Christ is the only way to God, I understand that millions of well-educated people emphatically reject what I believe. Either they don't believe it, or they doubt it, or they believe something else, or they would simply rather not be bothered by questions about God.

At this point in my life (I am in my mid-forties) I find myself spending many hours thinking about what I believe and why I believe it. In particular, I have focused on those doctrines of Christianity that can properly be called supernatural. Is there a God? How can we know? What does it mean to say the Bible is the Word of God? Who is Jesus Christ? Did He really rise from the dead? What does it mean to say that God created all things? What about angels and demons? Is Jesus really coming back to the earth, and if so, when?

I am happy not only to state what I believe, but to look at the reasons underlying those beliefs. In putting my thoughts on paper, I hope to provide some positive help to others (either spiritual seekers or fellow believers) who wonder about these same issues.

One word of caution: If you're not disposed to believe in Jesus, nothing in this book will convince you to change your mind. Since spiritual reality is a matter of perception and not proof, I don't believe in trying to argue people into the Kingdom of God. The Bible clearly says that no one can come to God unless the Father draws him through the Spirit (John 6:44; 16:8-11). So if you're a skeptic, don't fear—you won't be converted against your will by reading this book.

But that's only one side of the story. In his first letter Peter exhorts his readers to "always be prepared to give an answer to everyone who asks you to give the reason for the hope that you have" (1 Peter 3:15). Fair enough. Those of us who claim to know

Jesus Christ through faith ought to be ready with solid answers to honest questions. For that matter, we should also be ready to say, "I don't know" when we don't know. We have at various times hurt ourselves both ways—by refusing to answer and by answering beyond our knowledge.

Go back to the Gospels and you will discover that Jesus always answered His critics. Always. He answered everybody who came to Him, including the skeptical Sadducees and the hostile Pharisees. It was Socrates who said, "The unexamined life is not worth living." I think we could rephrase that to say, "The unexamined faith is not worth believing."

A quick word about the format. This book is organized into nine chapters covering the major areas of the Christian faith. Each chapter ends with a quote to think about, a few questions to ponder, and three Scripture passages to study.

There are several ways to read the book. Straight through— which won't take very long. Or one chapter at a time—better because you'll spend time thinking about the concepts. Or you might study this book with a few friends—best because then you can discuss the questions at the end of each chapter and come to your own conclusions.

All beliefs should be open to question. I've already said that I agree with that statement, but perhaps one word should be added. Perpetual searching for the truth can sometimes be an excuse not to make up your own mind.

In the pages that follow you will be invited to join me in a search for the truth, and in the end you will be invited to make up your own mind.

One

Best-seller and More

What a Christian Believes About the Bible

We begin with the simple observation that the Bible is the best-selling book of all time. More copies have been printed in more languages and read by more people than any other book in history. It is so far out in front of every other book ever written that it stands in a category all by itself. It is not only the best-selling religious book—it is the best-selling book of any and every category. The Bible is number one. The all-time best-seller. The undisputed champion.

Every week it is read, studied, quoted, and memorized in every nation on every continent. The Bible has now been translated into every major language of the world, and work goes on around the clock to translate it into out-of-the-way tribal languages that do not yet have it.

So if we had no other reason to study the Bible, it's unparalleled popularity must cause us to stop and consider it carefully. But the title of this chapter is "Best-seller *and More*." The question might be put this way: Why is the Bible still the all-time best-selling book in world history? What is it about this ancient book that still draws the attention of this generation? Why are we still attracted to these ancient stories? Is it just our religious background? Do we turn to the Bible because it makes us feel good in times of trouble? Or is there something more?

EVERY WORD AND ALL THE WORDS

Indeed there is something more, and it is the burden of this chapter to explain the "something more" about the Bible. For 2,000 years Christians have used a particular phrase to describe what they believe about the Bible. We call it *the Word of God*. That alone sets the Bible apart from every other book. When we use the phrase *the Word of God*, we mean that the Bible comes from God and records His message to us. That is, when we read the Bible, we are reading the very words of God. Sometimes Christians use the word *inspiration* to describe this truth. Second Timothy 3:16 tells us, "All Scripture is God-breathed." *That means God breathed out the very words of the Bible, and the human authors wrote them down.* Note three implications of this truth:

1. Inspiration extends to *every part* of the Bible.
2. Inspiration extends to the *very words* of the Bible.
3. Inspiration guarantees the *absolute truthfulness* of the Bible.
   The Bible is *infallible* (teaching only the truth).
   The Bible is *inerrant* (incapable of teaching error).

That in a nutshell is what we believe about the Bible. It is what we mean when we use the phrase *the Word of God*. But saying it is so doesn't make it so. Why do we believe the Bible is the Word of God and thus absolutely truthful? How can we be so sure that the Bible stands above every other book ever written? In this chapter we're going to attempt to answer those questions.

Let's suppose that someone comes up to you and offers you a soft drink you've never had before. No doubt you'll ask a few questions before you take a sip. You want to know its *claims* (what's on the label), its *credibility* (what's behind it), its *consistency* (what's in it), and its *certainty* or *effects* (what comes from drinking it). Let's apply those four tests to the Bible and see what we find.

ITS CLAIMS

In the first place, the Bible clearly claims to be the Word of God. Second Peter 1:21 says, "For prophecy never had its origin in the will of man, but men spoke from God as they were carried along by the Holy Spirit." It's not as if Jeremiah dreamed up his visions or David his psalms or Paul his letters. These men "spoke from God" as the Holy Spirit carried them along. The Greek word translated "carried along" pictures a ship being moved through the waters by the power of the wind in its sails. *The Holy Spirit is the real power behind the writing of the Bible.* He is the divine author; men like David, Daniel, and John were human authors. That's why the Bible repeatedly uses phrases like "the Lord says" and "the Word of the Lord came" and "the Lord spoke." Jeremiah 1:9 puts it very plainly: "Then the LORD reached out his hand and touched my mouth and said to me, 'Now, I have put my words in your mouth.'" This is a claim to direct, divine inspiration by God. In Galatians 1:11-12, Paul says that his message did not come from man but by direct revelation from God.

The writers of the Bible did not decide to sit down one day and write the Bible. Peter and Paul and Moses didn't get inspired or "on a roll" like Shakespeare writing his plays or John Grisham writing his novels![1] They were working in the power of the Holy Spirit who superintended the whole process to ensure the accuracy of everything they wrote. Paul Little offers this helpful clarification:

> It is important to realize too that the writers of the Scripture were not mere writing machines. God did not punch them like keys on a typewriter to produce His message. He did not dictate the words, as the biblical view of inspiration has so often been unfairly caricatured. It is quite clear that each writer has a style of his own. Jeremiah does not write like Isaiah, and John does not write like Paul. God worked through the instrumentality of human personality, but so guided and controlled men that what they wrote is what He wanted written.[2]

Whatever else we may say about the Bible, let's begin with what it says about itself. *The Bible claims to be the very Word of God.* It never pretends to be "just another book."

"So what if the Bible claims to be inspired by God? That doesn't make it so!" True. I could claim to be Jack Nicklaus, but that doesn't mean I could make a putt over two feet. *It's not the claim but what backs up the claim that counts.* Which brings us to the question of the Bible's credibility.

ITS CREDIBILITY

Let's consider credibility under two headings. First of all, *accuracy of transmission*. After all, everyone understands that the Bible was written 2,000 to 3,500 years ago. And everyone agrees that we don't possess any of the original manuscripts of the Bible. How do we know that what we are reading is an accurate transmission or translation of what the human authors originally wrote? The answer for the Old Testament is that the Jews were almost fanatical in their insistence on accuracy. When they copied a manuscript by hand, they counted the total number of letters and figured out the middle letter of the entire book. Once a scribe finished copying that book, if his middle letter of the copy was different, the entire book was presumed to be incorrectly copied and was destroyed. The scribes even counted the various letters and compared manuscripts, not just word for word but letter for letter. That's why all the existing manuscripts of the Old Testament are virtually identical.

We find the same accuracy of transmission in the New Testament. Scholars tell us that there are over 5,300 complete manuscripts of the New Testament (and another 8,000 partial manuscripts). And the oldest manuscripts go back to within a century of the original writings. Consider the following comparison. We have 5,300 manuscripts of the New Testament but no more than five for anything Aristotle wrote. And the earliest copy of Caesar's *Gallic Wars* dates 1,000 years after it was written. The first complete copy of Homer's *Odyssey* is dated 2,200 years after it was written.[3]

Let me say it plainly: The Bible is by far the best-attested ancient book in the world. There are more copies, earlier, and more accurately recorded than for any other book from ancient history.

Second, consider the Bible's *amazing historical accuracy*. In general, we see that historical research has tended to confirm every major factual claim in the Bible. For example, for many years the critics claimed that no one named Pontius Pilate ever existed—until archaeologists uncovered a stone tablet in Caesarea with his name on it. The Bible also mentioned a tribe of people (the Hittites) who the critics claimed never existed. But today scholars know that the Hittitte empire existed throughout the land we now call Turkey. The critics have been wrong about so many things. They claimed there was never a ruler named Belshazzar. They denied there was a king named Sargon. Both claims were proven wrong. Some radical scholars said the whole story of David was a myth, that there never was a King David at all. They said that because they couldn't find any contemporaneous proof. But several years ago, at a place called Tell Dan, archaeologists discovered an inscription that mentions the "House of David," which is the biblical term for David's kingdom.

On and on we could go, giving literally hundreds of examples where historical research and archaeological discoveries have confirmed the truth of the biblical record. Please understand—*I am not arguing that archaeology "proves" the Bible, but only that if the Bible is true, archaeology helps confirm that fact.*

We have nothing to fear from the closest scrutiny of the Bible. It will stand the test of any fair investigation.

ITS CONSISTENCY

Two important lines of evidence establish the Bible's internal consistency. First, there is the testimony of *fulfilled prophecy.* Someone has calculated that fully one-fourth of the Bible was prophecy when it was written. The sixty-six books of the Bible make hundreds of specific prophecies regarding people, places, kingdoms, wars, and nations. But the greatest evidence of predictive prophecy deals with the person of Jesus Christ. The Old Testament contains approximately 500 predictions regarding Christ, including the place of His birth, the manner of His birth, the family into which He would be born, the scope of His ministry, the nature of His death, and the miracle of His resurrection. All of these prophecies were written down between 400 and 1,500 years before His birth. Yet each of them was fulfilled down to the letter. Mathematician Peter Stoner calculated the odds of anyone fulfilling just eight of those predictions by chance. The odds came out to one in ten to the seventh power. That's one in 100 quadrillion! If you took that many silver dollars and scattered them across Texas, they would cover the state two feet deep. Now take one of those silver dollars, mark it with a red X, and throw it at random into that pile of silver dollars. Then blindfold a volunteer and ask him to find the marked silver dollar on his first try. That's the same odds that eight predictions about Christ could be fulfilled by chance. Yet Christ fulfilled over 500 prophecies![4]

Second, consider *the amazing unity of the Bible*. We are accustomed to thinking of the Bible as one book, but it also consists of sixty-six books written by forty authors over a period of 1,600 years. Yet the Bible is indeed *one book* because it contains an amazing unity in its theme from Genesis to Revelation.

How do we explain the unity of the Bible? The Old Testament points to the *coming* of Christ, the Gospels to the *appearance* of Christ, Acts to the *preaching* of Christ, the epistles to the *Body* of Christ (the true church), and Revelation to the *return* of Christ. Jesus Christ is the theme of the entire Bible. This amazing unity amid diversity is one of the great proofs of the Bible's supernatural origin.

ITS CERTAINTY

Having said all that, how can we be sure the Bible is the Word of God? Consider please one more line of evidence: *the evidence of changed lives*. History tells us that wherever the Bible goes, men and women are changed forever. It has transformed whole cultures from devil-worship, cannibalism, and warfare into societies in which human life is respected and human dignity established. If you doubt this, ask any missionary what happens when the Gospel is preached. I have listened to the people of Paraguay praise God in the Guarani language. I have seen with my own eyes young people in Haiti come to Christ and be set free from witchcraft and demonism. I have worshiped in Russian churches with believers who were persecuted for their faith by the Communists. I have met converts from Hinduism at a church in Nepal. I attended a service in Jerusalem with nearly 500 believers, many of them Messianic Jews. Everywhere the Bible is preached, it radically changes hearts, lives, families, cities, cultures, and entire nations.

IRONSIDE AND THE AGNOSTIC

You may question the Bible if you like, but you cannot deny its power to transform the human heart. Early in his ministry, Harry Ironside was living in the San Francisco Bay area, working with the Brethren assemblies there. One evening as he was walking through the city, he came upon a group of Salvation Army workers holding a meeting on the corner of Market and Grant Avenues. When they recognized Ironside, they asked him to give his testimony. So he did, telling how God had saved him through faith in the literal, bodily death and resurrection of Jesus Christ.

As he was speaking, he noticed on the edge of the crowd a well-dressed man who had taken a card from his pocket and was writing something on it. As Ironside finished his talk, the man came forward, lifted his hat, and very politely handed him the card. On one side was the man's name, which Ironside immediately recognized, for he was one of the early Socialists who had made a name for himself lecturing not only *for* socialism but *against* Christianity. As Ironside turned the card over, he read, "Sir, I challenge you to debate with me the question 'Agnosticism versus Christianity' in the Academy of Science Hall next Sunday afternoon at four o'clock. I will pay all expenses."

Ironside read the card aloud and then replied, in essence, "I am very much interested in this challenge. I will be glad to agree to this debate on the following conditions: namely, that in order to prove that this gentleman has something worth debating about, he will promise to bring with him to the lecture hall next Sunday two people, whose qualifications I will give in a moment, as proof that agnosticism is of real value in changing human lives and building true character.

"First, he must promise to bring with him one man who was for years what we commonly call a 'down-and-outer.' I am not particular as to the exact nature of the sins that wrecked his life and made him an outcast from society—whether a drunkard, or a criminal of some kind, or a victim of his sensual appetite. But it must be a man who for years was under the power of evil habits from which he could not deliver himself. Then on some occasion he entered one of this man's meetings and heard his glorification of agnosticism and his denunciations of the Bible and Christianity. As he listened to such an address he was so deeply stirred that he went away from that meeting saying, 'Henceforth, I too am an agnostic!' And as a result of imbibing that particular philosophy he found that a new power had come into his life. The sins he once loved he now hates, and righteousness and goodness are now the ideals of his life. He is now an entirely new man, a credit to himself, and an asset to society—all because he is an agnostic.

"Secondly, I would like my opponent to promise to bring with him one woman who was once a poor, hopeless outcast, the slave of evil passions and the victim of man's corrupt living, utterly lost, ruined, and wretched because of her life of sin. But this woman also entered a hall where this man was loudly proclaiming his agnosticism and ridiculing the message of the Holy Scriptures. As she listened, hope was born in her heart, and she said, 'This is just what I need to deliver me from the slavery of sin!' She followed this man's teaching and became an intelligent agnostic or infidel. As a result, her whole being revolted against the degradation of the life she had been living. She fled from the den of iniquity where she had been held captive for so long; and today, rehabilitated, she has won her way back to an honored position in society and is living a clean, virtuous, happy life—all because she is an agnostic.

"Now," he said, addressing the man who had presented him with his card and the challenge, "if you will promise to bring these two people with you as examples of what agnosticism can do, I will promise to meet you at the Academy of Science Hall at four o'clock next Sunday, and I will bring with me at the very least 100 men and women who for years lived in just such sinful degradation as I have tried to depict, but who have been gloriously saved through believing the Gospel that you ridicule. I will have these men and women with me on the platform as witnesses to the miraculous saving power of Jesus Christ and as present-day proof of the truth of the Bible."

Dr. Ironside then turned to the Salvation Army captain, a young woman, and said, "Captain, have you any who could go with me to such a meeting?" She exclaimed with enthusiasm, "We can give you forty at least, just from this one corps, and we will give you a brass band to lead the procession!"

"Fine," Dr. Ironside answered. "Now, sir, I will have no difficulty picking up sixty others from the various missions, gospel halls, and evangelical churches of the city. So if you will promise to bring two such exhibits as I have described, I will come marching in at the head of such a procession, with the band playing 'Onward, Christian Soldiers,' and I will be ready for the debate."

Apparently the man who had made the challenge had a sense of humor, for he smiled wryly and waved his hand in a deprecating kind of way as if to say "Nothing doing!" and then edged out of the crowd while the bystanders applauded Ironside and the others.[5]

YOU STILL HAVE TO MAKE UP YOUR MIND

Is the Bible the Word of God? I cannot "prove" that to you. You still have to make up your own mind. But if you have doubts, I encourage you to read it for yourself, study its claims, observe its message, and check out the facts for yourself. I have done that, and I have also read the claims of the skeptics. As for me and my house, we will stand on the Bible as the Word of God.

I submit to you that the Bible will stand the toughest test, the hardest scrutiny, because it is indeed the Word of God. That's why after 2,000 years it is still the world's best-seller. No other book contains the plan of salvation. No other book can tell you how to get to heaven.

THE BIBLE TELLS ME SO

One Sunday after I had finished preaching, a young girl pressed some paper into my hand. She said she had written something as a gift to me. When I looked at it later, it turned out to be a little handwritten book called "God really does love us." The first page is a drawing of a cross with a heart and the sun shining upon it. The caption reads, "God loves us!" The second page shows a young girl kneeling before Jesus on the cross. She is telling Him she loves Him. The final page, showing Jesus on the cross, has the words, "God really did die for me!" Where did she learn such truth? I think I know the answer. Many years ago most of us learned to sing a little song that goes like this:

> *Jesus loves me, this I know, for the Bible tells me so.*
> *Little ones to Him belong, they are weak, but He is strong.*
> *Yes, Jesus loves me. Yes Jesus loves me.*
> *Yes, Jesus loves me. The Bible tells me so.*[6]

Indeed it does. *Thank God for the Bible because without it, we would never know about Jesus. And without Jesus, we could never be saved.* The Bible is true, and it is the Word of God. If you still have doubts, I

encourage you to read it for yourself. When you do, you will discover for yourself the most wonderful truth in the world: Yes, Jesus
loves us. The Bible tells us so.

SOMETHING TO THINK ABOUT

The secret of my success? It is simple. It is found in the Bible, "In
all thy ways acknowledge Him and He shall direct thy paths."
—GEORGE WASHINGTON CARVER

QUESTIONS TO CONSIDER

1. What does it mean to call the Bible *the Word of God*?

2. How would you explain the concept of inerrancy to someone
else?

3. Which "proof" of the Bible seems most important to you?

4. Can you think of any ways in which the message of the Bible
has changed your life? Why are some people not changed at all by
the message of the Bible?

5. What does it mean to say that the Bible is "inspired" by God?
Why is that concept crucial to our understanding?

6. What does fulfilled prophecy teach us about the Bible?
About Jesus Christ?

SCRIPTURES TO PONDER

Psalm 19:7-14

2 Timothy 3:16

Revelation 22:18-19

Two

THE ULTIMATE QUESTION

What a Christian Believes About God

Is belief in God nothing but superstition? Some people think so. The dictionary defines superstition as "a belief held despite evidence to the contrary." That definition reminds me of how one little boy defined faith: "Faith is believing what you know isn't true." In this chapter I want to tell you why belief in God is reasonable. I also want to sketch two aspects of the God Christians worship.

Before jumping in, however, I must issue one disclaimer. I do not believe I can "prove" God's existence in the absolute sense of that word. Either God exists or He doesn't. *If He does, then His existence ought to be the most obvious fact in the universe.* If He doesn't, that too should be obvious. However, I realize that some people will choose not to believe no matter what the evidence says. Just as a jury may choose to ignore overwhelming evidence, some individuals may choose to ignore the overwhelming evidence of God's existence.[1]

With that in mind, let's consider some reasons for believing in God.

GOD ACTUALLY EXISTS

Across the centuries theologians have developed various lines of argument regarding God's existence. These arguments (called the classical proofs) generally start with the universe as we know it and argue from what we know to what we don't know. They draw logical inferences in order to reach valid conclusions. Several of the arguments deserve our attention.

Argument from First Cause

This argument is sometimes called the cosmological argument or the argument from cause to effect. It begins with the simple observation that for everything that exists, there must be a cause that brought it into being. We cannot conceive of an effect that does not have a preceding cause. Fruit grows because someone planted the seed. A gust of wind causes the sailboat to knife through the waves. The sunshine causes the fog to evaporate. The lapping waves on the seashore wash away the sand castles. A man hits a few buttons and a phone rings on the other side of the world. And so it goes. For every effect there must be a cause that made it happen.

Now consider this: the universe itself—all of it—exists as the ultimate effect. Where or how did the universe come into being? If everything in the universe has a cause, what caused the universe in the first place? Think about that question for a moment. If everything in the universe operates according to the law of cause and effect, and if there are no known exceptions to this law, where did the universe come from? Who or what brought it into being?

Since the cause must be greater than the effect, the only explanation for the universe as we know it is that it was created by Someone who has infinite power. That Someone is God.

The universe is God's calling card. *Not just a part of the universe, but the universe as a whole speaks of God's existence.* This is what David meant when he proclaimed, "The heavens declare the glory of God; the skies proclaim the work of his hands" (Psalm 19:1). It's also what Paul meant when he wrote in Romans 1:20, "For since the creation of the world God's invisible qualities—his eternal power and divine nature—have been clearly seen, being understood from what has been made." His words are entirely unambiguous. The key phrase is "clearly seen." Paul means that the truth about God is so plain in nature that everyone sees it, everyone knows it, everyone understands several important facts simply by looking at creation. What are these indisputable facts?

- There is a God.
- He is a God of infinite power.
- He is a God of creative design.

Everyone knows these things because God has put His personal stamp on every single portion of the universe. *Only the willfully blind refuse to see it.* The only way to rationally explain the universe as we know it is the existence of an all-powerful, infinite, personal God—the God of the Bible.

The Argument from Design

This argument answers the question, "How do you account for the complexity of the universe?" It is sometimes called the watchmaker argument, in honor of William Paley who several hundred years ago said that if you saw a watch by the side of the road, even if you didn't know anything else, you would know the watch didn't assemble itself by chance. A watch demands a watchmaker. In the same way, the incredible complexity of our universe demands the existence of an intelligent designer who brought it all into being.

Suppose you visited Mt. Rushmore in South Dakota and exclaimed, "What an amazing feat of nature this is! What a coincidence that water and wind eroded the face of the mountain until it looks just like Washington, Jefferson, Lincoln, and Roosevelt." But when you pick up a brochure you discover that Mt. Rushmore is the work of a brilliant, visionary sculptor named Gutzon Borglum. When he looked at the uncut mountain, he "saw" the four presidents there, and from his vision came the monument we see today.

Recently I spoke at a Florida conference center where the flowers in one bed spelled out "God is love." Would a person looking at that say, "What a coincidence! Somehow those flowers just happened to grow in precisely the right places to spell out those words"? No; intelligent design demands an intelligent designer.

You either see that or you don't. Now, that doesn't prove God. But just as a watch points to a watchmaker, just as Mt. Rushmore points to a dedicated architect, just as *The Old Man and the Sea* points to Ernest Hemingway, the beauty and order and complexity of the universe point to Almighty God—the ultimate designer of all things.

Psalm 8:3 says, "When I consider the heavens, the work of your fingers, the moon and the stars, which you have set in place. . . ." God has left His fingerprints on the universe. Every rock, every tree, every river, every ocean, every star in the sky—they all bear the divine DNA that points back to the God who created all things.

The Argument from Man's Religious Nature

Man is incurably religious. Anthropologists tell us that even among the remotest tribes, no matter how primitive, there is a belief in God, a universal spirit, or some form of higher power.

But what about modern man? Surely, some say, he has progressed to the point where belief in God is unnecessary. Hardly. A poll by the *Chicago Sun-Times* reveals just the opposite. An overwhelming 94 percent of those surveyed answered yes to the question, "Do you believe in God?"[2] That figure is consistent with results from around the country. Despite years of secularization in the public media and the rise of an active humanist movement, the vast majority of Americans still believe in God. Even people who rarely or never attend church believe in God. Some atheists even pray regularly, apparently hedging their bets!

Where does this nearly universal belief in God come from? Who put it inside the human heart? Is it only superstition, or perhaps the product of generations of religious training? Is it a quirk of uncompleted evolution?

The apostle Paul gives us the answer in Romans 2:14-15: "When Gentiles, who do not have the law, do by nature the things required by the law, they are a law for themselves . . . since they show that the requirements of the law are written on their hearts, their consciences also bearing witness." This explains why people have an innate sense of right and wrong. Even in societies that don't have or recognize the Ten Commandments, most people know by nature that it is wrong to commit murder (Exodus 20:13). They may not use the Bible's precise words, but they instinctively know that murder is wrong. The same is true of the other commandments—those against stealing, lying, adultery, and also the commandment commanding us to honor our parents. Atheists have no logical explanation for the existence of the moral conscience in every person's heart.

Perhaps you've heard of the "God-shaped vacuum" inside every human heart. Over 1,500 years ago St. Augustine said, "O Lord, you have made us for Yourself, and our hearts are restless until they find rest in You." King Solomon summarized the human condition with these words: "He [God] has set eternity in the hearts of men" (Ecclesiastes 3:11). There is an emptiness and a longing for God inside every human heart, and only God can fill that emptiness and satisfy that longing.

GOD IS A TRINITY

The doctrine of the Trinity has been called both the most puzzling doctrine in the Christian faith and the central truth of the Christian faith. Which is it? Inscrutable puzzle or central truth? The answer is, both.

This doctrine unites all true Christians and also serves as a line of demarcation between genuine Christians and followers of other religions. You may believe in the Trinity and still not be a Christian; but if you deny this doctrine in your heart, you are not a Christian at all. Having said that, I admit that no one fully understands it. It is a mystery and a paradox. Yet I believe it is true.

I can think of at least three reasons for believing in the Trinity.

- The Bible teaches this doctrine.
- Christians everywhere have always believed it.
- No other explanation makes sense.

Someone has said it this way: If you try to explain the Trinity, you will lose your mind. But if you deny it, you will lose your soul.

Here is a series of statements that explains what Christians mean when they say God is a Trinity:

- There is one God and only one.
- He exists in three persons.
- The three are equal and eternal.
- The three are worthy of equal praise and worship.
- The three are distinct yet act in unity.
- The three constitute the one true God of the Bible.

As you might imagine, the early church struggled mightily over this doctrine. They eventually reduced their belief in the Trinity to two short statements. They concluded that God is:

- One in essence.
- Three in person.

When we say these things, we mean that the Father is God, the Son is God, and the Holy Spirit is God; yet, they are not three gods but only one God. The Father is not the Son, the Son is not the Spirit, and the Spirit is not the Father. But each is God individually; and together They are the one true God of the Bible.

If asked for biblical proof of this doctrine, we can point out that all three persons are called God in different places in the Bible.

- *The Father*—Galatians 1:1.
- *The Son*—John 20:28.
- *The Spirit*—Acts 5:3-4.

How could the Son and the Spirit be called God unless They somehow share in God's essence? But if They share in God's essence, They are God alongside the Father.

We also find all three persons associated together on an equal basis in numerous passages:

- Jesus' baptism—Matthew 3:13-17.
- Salvation—1 Peter 1:2.
- Benediction—2 Corinthians 13:14.
- Christian baptism—Matthew 28:19.
- Prayer—Ephesians 3:14-21.
- Christian growth/sanctification—2 Thessalonians 2:13.

This list of passages could easily be extended. It simply shows how easily the writers of Scripture passed from one person of the Trinity to another, doing so in a way that assumes Their equality of nature while preserving Their distinct personhood. If the doctrine of the Trinity is not true, it would seem to be blasphemy to speak so freely of the Father, the Son, and the Holy Spirit in one and the same breath.

The doctrine of the Trinity also helps us answer the question, "What was God doing before He created the universe?" This is a question little children like to stump their parents with. But skeptics like to ask it as well. Augustine's answer was, "He was preparing hell for people who ask questions like that!" The doctrine of the Trinity teaches us that before the foundation of the world, God was having fellowship within His own being. That's why the Bible tells us that the

Father loves the Son (John 17:26). In some sense we can never understand, God the Father, God the Son, and God the Holy Spirit have forever communicated and loved each other. This also teaches us that God is never lonely. He didn't create us because He "needed" us. God could have existed forever without us. That He made us at all is a statement of His great love and the wisdom of His plan.

Seeing that God is a Trinity also helps us understand what really happened at the cross. At the climax of Jesus' suffering, He cried out, "My God, my God, why have you forsaken me?" (Matthew 27:46). What do those strange, tortured words mean? We have a hint of the answer in that every other time Jesus prayed, He used the term *Father*. But at the moment when He bore the full weight of the sins of the world, when all that is evil and wretched was poured out upon Him in some way we cannot begin to fathom, God—who cannot look upon sin—turned His back on His own Son. Sin, as it were (though not in ultimate reality), caused a rupture in the Trinity. Instead of "Father," Jesus cried out, "My God, my God!" This is God speaking to God. The eternal Son cried out to the Father at the moment when the penalty of sin was laid upon Him. Some might ask how one man could pay for the sins of the entire race, and we find the answer in the doctrine of the Trinity. Only an infinite God could bear the sins of the world

Someone asked Daniel Webster, who happened to be a fervent Christian, "How can a man of your intellect believe in the Trinity?" "I do not pretend fully to understand the arithmetic of heaven now," he replied. That's a good phrase—the arithmetic of heaven.

The fact of the Trinity should cause us to bow in humble adoration before a God who is greater than our minds could ever comprehend. We have a Triune God who has provided a trinitarian salvation. When we were lost in sin, our God acted in every person of His being to save us. The Father gave the Son, the Son offered Himself on the cross, and the Holy Spirit brought us to Jesus. We were so lost that it took every member of the Godhead to save us.

GOD IS GRACIOUS

Our discussion of the Trinity and our salvation leads directly to the doctrine of God's grace. Why do we need grace? Because all men and all women are by nature spiritually dead and separated from God. We must begin at this precise point in order to understand what grace really means. Ephesians 2:1 tells us, "You were dead in your transgressions and sins."

This is God's indictment of the entire human race apart from His grace. We tend to dismiss these words as not literally true. After all, how dead can we really be? We don't *look* dead. To our eyes, we look very alive. Not so. God says that apart from His grace, all men are dead.

The Bible says that apart from grace the whole human race, and each one of us individually, is spiritually dead, in rebellion against God, under God's judgment, guilty and unclean, and thus worthy of eternal damnation. We are not simply unworthy of heaven apart from God's grace—we are entirely worthy of hell. This is what God says about you and me. It is also what God says about your husband or wife, your children, your parents, your grandparents, your uncles, your aunts, your neighbors, your friends, your classmates, and your business associates.

Let me illustrate this. Imagine that while you are walking down the street you happen upon a corpse. While you stop to ponder who this is, someone drags a second corpse and places it next to the first one. This puzzles you, but before you can ask any questions, three more corpses are thrown onto the first two. Suddenly from every side corpses are being tossed upon the pile. Old and young, rich and poor, black and white, men and women—they seem to be coming from every direction. You step back and watch as the pile grows before your eyes. In a matter of seconds, it becomes a mountain of stinking corpses. Soon the mountain reaches to the skies with more dead bodies being added by the second.

According to Ephesians 2, that is what God sees when he looks down from heaven. Not our supposed good deeds, not our vaunted achievements, not our fame or our wealth. God sees death on every side. He sees dead men walking.

Now suppose you ask, which corpse deserves to be brought back to life? The answer is, it doesn't matter—they all stink. Dead is dead. That leads us to another important truth. God is not obliged to save anyone. Or to show mercy to anyone. Or to forgive anyone. God would be perfectly justified in letting the dead stay dead.

It is at this point that the meaning of grace becomes clear. Ephesians 2:4-5 uses three words to describe how God saves sinners: "love, mercy, grace." *Love* is the attribute of God that causes Him to reach out to His creatures in benevolence. *Mercy* is God's withholding punishment. *Grace* is the unmerited favor of God.

Think of it this way. God's love begins as a vast reservoir in His heart. As it begins to flow toward us, it becomes a river of mercy. As it cascades down upon us, the mercy becomes a torrent of grace.

Two key words always go together: *Free grace*. Some might call this a "blessed redundancy." And so it is, because if grace isn't free, it isn't grace. If you have to pay for it, work for it, or do anything to earn it, it's not grace because it's not free.

Ephesians 2:6-9 tells us what God's grace does for sinners. Because of His undeserved kindness, they are:

- "Raised" (verse 6).
- "Seated" (verse 6).
- "Saved" (verse 8).

That says it all. He takes dead men and *raises* them. He takes enslaved men and *seats* them with Christ in heaven. He takes condemned men and *saves* them from judgment. Grace is thus God's total answer to the moral ruin of the human race. It is such a complete answer that nothing else could ever be added to it.

THE BEST ARGUMENT
FOR GOD'S EXISTENCE

When all is said and done, I believe the best argument for the Christian view of God is found in the person of Jesus Christ. When you consider the amazing prophecies of the Old Testament that foretold every major detail of His life and death, when you consider the record of His ministry, the stories He told, the miracles He performed, and the exemplary life He lived, you must conclude that He was more than a man—He was the Son of God.

I would also submit that the ultimate proof of God centers around the death, burial, and resurrection of Jesus Christ. Therefore, when talking with an atheist I recommend that you not spend much time on the classical proofs. Rather, focus on Jesus Christ. Who was He? How do you account for Him?

BREAKFAST WITH AN ATHEIST

Not long ago I had breakfast with an atheist. It turned out to be a most enlightening experience. Although we were meeting for the first time, I immediately came to appreciate his many positive qualities. He was charming, friendly, positive, talkative, and obviously very well-educated. Sometime during his college years, he had abandoned not only the Christian faith but his belief in God. He actually converted from Christianity to atheism. He truly believes there is no God. As we talked, he kept emphasizing that only this life has meaning. Since there is no life after death, what we do now becomes vitally important. Heaven for him is just a myth that religious people use to comfort themselves in times of trouble. We had a long talk, and I learned a great deal from him. It's always useful to see yourself as others see you.

I came away from our time together with three fundamental observations:

- How difficult it is to be an atheist.
- How hard an atheist must work to keep his "faith."
- How careful an atheist must be lest he start believing in God.

Toward the end of our time together, I asked him what he thought about Jesus Christ. He seemed a bit surprised by that question, as if it had no relevance to the question of God's existence. It was my turn to be surprised when he told me that he hadn't thought about Jesus very much one way or the other. He then ventured to say that Jesus was probably a great man and a learned teacher, but He probably never meant to start a religion. That happened after He died; His followers just wanted to honor His memory.

Upon hearing that, I decided to press the point. What about His resurrection? What if He really did rise from the dead? My friend stopped for a moment, thought a bit, and then a smile crossed his face. "Well, we'd have a problem then, wouldn't we?" Exactly! If Jesus really did rise from the dead, then He really is the Son of God, and God really does exist.

That's what I mean when I say that Jesus is the best proof of God's existence. In our witnessing we should bring people back again and again to Jesus Christ. He is the ultimate argument for God because He was in fact God in human flesh. "In the beginning was the Word, and the Word was with God, and the Word was God. . . . The Word became flesh and lived for a while among us" (John 1:1, 14).

I close with this simple statement: Not only does it make sense to believe in God, it makes no sense not to.

- No fact is so obvious as the fact of God's existence.
- You must deny reality itself in order to deny God's existence.
- The atheist must stand on ground God created in order to deny God.

I submit to you that the evidence for God's existence is overwhelming. But it still demands a choice. In one of his books Anthony Campolo tells how he shares the Gospel with secular-minded university students who ask him why he believes the Bible. "Because I decided to," he replies. Then he asks the student, "Why don't you believe the Bible?" The answer is almost always the same: "I guess because I decided not to."[3]

After all the arguments on both sides are finished, you still have to decide for yourself. You still have to choose. *What choice have you made?*

I believe in God because without Him nothing in this universe makes sense. God exists; He is real, and Jesus Christ is His Son. He knows you, and He loves you, and He gave His only begotten Son so that you might be saved. What do you think about that?

SOMETHING TO THINK ABOUT

Pascal says there are three kinds of people: those who have sought God and found him, those who are seeking and have not yet found, and those who neither seek nor find. The first are reasonable and happy, the second are reasonable and unhappy, the third are both unreasonable and unhappy.

—PETER KREEFT AND RON TACELLI

QUESTIONS TO CONSIDER

1. Do you agree that belief in God is nothing but superstition? If you disagree, how would you explain your own belief in God?

2. Why is the Trinity so hard to understand? How would you illustrate it to someone else? Do you agree that the Trinity is a fundamental doctrine of the Christian faith?

3. Apart from God's grace, all people are a) basically good, or b) both good and bad, or c) critically ill because of sin, or d) spiritually dead. Defend your answer.

4. What truths about God can be discovered by studying the universe around us? How do unbelievers explain the complexity and evidence of intelligent design in nature?

5. Do you agree there is a "God-shaped vacuum" inside every person? Who put it there? What happens when we don't fill that vacuum with God?

6. "It makes no sense not to believe in God." Do you agree? Why or why not?

SCRIPTURES TO PONDER

Psalm 19:1-6
Romans 1:18-21
Romans 11:33-36

Three

LORD, LIAR, OR LUNATIC

What a Christian Believes About Jesus Christ

Who is Jesus Christ? Before you answer that question, let me set the scene. It's a few minutes past noon in downtown San Antonio. You're walking with a few friends to a favorite lunch spot when a camera crew stops you for a spontaneous interview. To your surprise, their questions have nothing to do with the White House, politics, the economy, or where you stand on capital punishment. The interviewer wants to know what you think about Jesus Christ. Who is He?

While you fumble for an answer, the video camera records your discomfort. You weren't prepared to be quizzed on theology while your friends watch from five feet away. The seconds pass as various answers flash across your mental screen: "A good man . . . the Son of God . . . a prophet . . . a Galilean rabbi . . . a teacher of God's Law . . . the embodiment of God's love . . . a reincarnated spirit master . . . the ultimate revolutionary . . . the Messiah of Israel . . . Savior . . . a first-century wise man . . . a man just like any other man . . . King of kings . . . a misunderstood teacher . . . Lord of the universe . . . a fool who thought he was God's Son . . . the Son of Man . . . a fabrication of the early church."

Which answer will you give? Before you answer, let me say that various people today give all of those possible answers. Does that surprise you? It shouldn't. It's said that in the days before Elvis Presley died, he had been reading a book called *The Many Faces of Jesus.* That title stands as a fitting symbol of the confusion surrounding Jesus in our time. Two thousand years have passed, and we still wonder about the man called Jesus.

But that's nothing new. When Jesus asked His disciples, "Who do people say the Son of Man is?" they replied with four different answers (see Matthew 16:13-16). Even when He walked on this earth, people were confused as to His true identity. Some thought He was a prophet, others a great political leader, still others that He was John the Baptist come back to life.

One question with many answers. One man with many faces.

Who is Jesus Christ? And why do Christians believe in Him? As we begin our search for the answers, let's start by surveying some modern-day versions of Jesus.

MODERN VERSIONS OF JESUS

The Good Man

We start with this view because it is no doubt the most popular "face" of Jesus. Ask any ten nonreligious people on the street who Jesus is, and eight of them will say something like, "He was a good man who lived a long time ago." People who say such things do not pretend to be Bible scholars in any sense of the word, nor do they mean to be offensive. They are simply reflecting the common wisdom most of us learned as children: When in doubt, say something nice.

Of all the modern versions of Christ, this one is both the closest to the truth and the deadliest error. Jesus *was* a good man. Acts 10:38 says, "He went around doing good," referring to His miracles. But to stop there is to miss the central truth of His divine personality. Yes, He was a good man! But only because He was also the Son of God who came from heaven to be the Savior of the world.

The Misunderstood Rabbi

People who hold this view see Jesus as a talented Jewish teacher who never meant to start a new religion. They see Him as a first-century Martin Luther who wanted to reform Judaism but ended up being crucified for His efforts. Moreover, they don't believe He rose from the dead, but that His disciples believed He was present with them after His death, and thus the legend of the Resurrection arose in order to keep the dream alive.

The Revolutionary Jesus

This view was very popular in the sixties when left-wing radicals appropriated Jesus as the Messiah who came to overthrow the unjust power structures of His day and to bring in the Kingdom through protest and nonviolent action. Some theologians even used the image of the revolutionary Jesus to support the establishment of Marxist governments around the world.

Thankfully, we don't hear much about this nowadays. Ever since the collapse of communism and the fall of the Berlin Wall, the revolutionary Jesus has become a relic of modern history. As many people have pointed out, Jesus was indeed a revolutionary, but not in the sense intended by those who used the term. *Jesus came to start a revolution of love on Planet Earth.* He wasn't concerned about overthrowing governments but about overthrowing sin in the human heart.

The Ecumenical Christ

This is the option for people who like Jesus but don't want to worship Him exclusively. They lump Him together with other notable religious leaders such as Moses, Confucius, Gandhi, Buddha, and Mohammed. Such people have a Mt. Rushmore religion. When they look up, they see four or five faces peering down from heaven, and Jesus is one of the faces they see. Pick the one you like and worship him. Many people believe in the ecumenical Christ because it's a convenient way to call yourself a Christian and still be open-minded about other options.

After surveying the various answers of modern man, we are still left with the great question of history: "Who is Jesus Christ?" If those answers are wrong, what is the right answer, and how can we be sure?

THE GREAT QUESTION OF HISTORY

In order to answer that question, we have to go back to the New Testament, which is the only reliable source of information about Jesus Christ. It's true that we do have some information about Jesus in extra-biblical sources from the first century, but it is limited and scattered. *The only way to get an accurate picture of Jesus is to study the record of His life found in the four Gospels.* When we do, five important facts emerge that form the answer to history's greatest question.

Fact #1: Fulfilled Prophecy

The Bible uses a fascinating phrase to describe the moment of Jesus' birth. That phrase is: "the fulness of the time" (Galatians 4:4, *King James Version*). It refers to that one chosen moment in history when God arranged all the circumstances perfectly so that His Son would be born in just the right way at just the right moment at the precisely chosen location. That phrase also refers to the all the circumstances of His life, including His death and resurrection. All of this was perfectly planned by God and was predicted in writing before it happened.

Consider this: The Bible predicted all of the following about Jesus Christ before He was born:

- He would be born of a virgin—Isaiah 7:14.
- He would be born in Bethlehem—Micah 5:2.
- He would be born into the tribe of Judah—Genesis 49:10.
- His ministry would begin in Galilee—Isaiah 9:1.
- He would work miracles—Isaiah 35:5-6.
- He would teach in parables—Psalm 78:2.
- He would enter Jerusalem on a donkey—Zechariah 9:9.
- He would be betrayed by a friend—Psalm 41:9.
- He would be sold for thirty pieces of silver—Zechariah 11:12.
- He would be accused by false witnesses—Psalm 35:11.
- He would be wounded and bruised—Isaiah 53:5.
- His hands and feet would be pierced—Psalm 22:16.

- He would be crucified with sinful men—Isaiah 53:12.
- His garments would be torn apart and lots cast for them—Psalm 22:18.
- None of His bones would be broken—Psalm 34:20.
- His side would be pierced—Zechariah 12:10.
- He would be buried in a rich man's tomb—Isaiah 53:9.
- He would rise from the dead—Psalm 16:10.

These are only a few of the *hundreds* of prophecies about Jesus Christ in the Old Testament. The amount of detail in this list is striking. Even a casual reader must admit that either this is an amazing coincidence or it is the result of divine planning.

Fact #2: Amazing Claims

Here is a fact not often appreciated by the nonreligious person: Jesus made absolutely astounding claims concerning Himself. In fact, if you catalog His own words, you must conclude that either He is who He said He is or else He is a liar or a madman. The people who say, "Jesus was a good man—nothing more" have never read the Gospels because you could never come to that conclusion if you actually read what Jesus said about Himself.

For instance:
- He claimed to be the Son of God.
  "For God so loved the world that he gave his one and only Son" *(John 3:16).*
- He claimed that the angels obeyed Him.
  "The Son of Man will send out his angels" *(Matthew 13:41).*
- He claimed to be the ultimate judge of all men.
  "The Father . . . has entrusted all judgment to the Son" *(John 5:22).*

- He claimed to possess all power in heaven and on earth.
  "All authority in heaven and on earth has been given to me"
  (Matthew 28:18).

- He claimed to have the power to forgive sin.
  "Friend, your sins are forgiven" (Luke 5:20).

- He claimed that He could raise people from the dead.
  "All who are in their graves will hear his voice and come out" (John
  5:28-29).

- He claimed that He could raise Himself from the dead.
  "I have the authority to lay it [His life] down and authority to take
  it up again" (John 10:18).

- He claimed to be one with God.
  "I and the Father are one" (John 10:30).

- He claimed to be the only way to God.
  "No one comes to the Father except through me" (John 14:6).

- He claimed to be the giver of eternal life.
  "I give them eternal life" (John 10:28).

Before we go any further, let us note that these are absolutely stupendous claims. What would you do if your neighbor knocked on your door and said, "I am God's Son, and I can raise myself from the dead"? I daresay that you would close the door and call the police because anyone who goes around talking like that is likely to be a danger to himself and possibly to others.[1] But Jesus routinely made such claims about Himself. Laugh if you will, but before you dismiss Him, consider what He had to say.

Fact #3: Supernatural Power

When John the Baptist was in prison, he sent his disciples to Jesus with a very poignant question: "Are you the one who was to come, or should we expect someone else?" (Matthew 11:3). Jesus answered by listing the miracles He had performed: the blind could see, the lame could walk, the deaf could hear, the lepers were cleansed, and the dead were raised. No one could fake such miracles as that. No religious charlatan could give sight to the blind. Not even the great Houdini could raise the dead. Only the mighty Son of God could work such stupendous miracles.

Let me highlight some of Jesus' miracles:

- He turned water into wine (John 2:1-11).
- He multiplied the loaves and fishes (John 6:5-13).
- He walked on water (Matthew 14:25).
- He opened the eyes of the blind (John 9).
- He made the lame walk (Matthew 9:1-8).
- He cast out demons (Mark 5:1-20).
- He stilled a raging storm (Mark 4:35-41).
- He cleansed ten lepers (Luke 17:11-19).
- He raised the dead (Matthew 9:18-26).

Not long ago I read about a televangelist who made extravagant claims for healing that have now evidently been exposed as fraudulent. Sadly, this is not unusual these days. Anyone can claim to work miracles. *But only Jesus can do it!* His life was marked by miraculous power—which is exactly what you would expect from the Son of God.

Fact #4: The Empty Tomb

This, of course, is the ultimate proof. It is also the ultimate question. *Did Jesus really rise from the dead?* If He did, then He really was the

Son of God. If He didn't, then He's not the Son of God. In fact, if He didn't, He's not even a good man but rather the world's greater faker. And we are fools for following Him.

Therefore, I invite you to study the Gospels with an unprejudiced mind and to come to your own conclusions. When you do, I believe you will find the following four statements to be absolutely true.

- Jesus was really dead.
- Jesus was buried in a tomb.
- The tomb was empty on Sunday morning.
- Jesus appeared to His disciples after the Resurrection, alive from the dead.

In the years following the French Revolution, there was a great turning away from Christianity. A man named La Revilliere concocted a new religion that he fancied to be superior to Christianity. Unfortunately, he had trouble gaining converts. So he went to the great diplomat Charles de Talleyrand for help. Talleyrand's advice was simple: "To ensure success for your new religion, all you need to do is have yourself crucified and then rise again from the dead on the third day."[2]

The man's religion disappeared because he was unable to follow Talleyrand's advice. *Only one person ever has—Jesus our Lord.* The story of His death and resurrection is perhaps the best-attested fact of ancient history.

The entire Christian faith hangs on this one fact: *Jesus rose from the dead—literally, physically, bodily, visibly.* The testimony of the empty tomb forever sets Jesus Christ apart from all other religious leaders. They are dead. But He is alive today.

Fact #5: Transformed Lives

Before you make a final decision about Jesus, there is one additional fact to consider. When Jesus left this earth 2,000 years ago, He left behind a few hundred disciples in Israel. That's all He had to show for His thirty-three years.

Today nearly two billion people have proudly borne His name. That tiny band of followers has spread to every nation on every continent. Thousands more join the ranks every single day. In fact, more people have come to Christ in the last generation than in the previous 2,000 years.

History shows that Jesus Christ continues to change lives twenty centuries after He walked the dusty roads of Galilee and braved the narrow cobblestone streets of Jerusalem. *Today He is the single most influential person in all of human history.* John Lennon is dead, Jerry Garcia is dead, Karl Marx is dead, Adolf Hitler is dead, Napoleon is dead. *But Jesus Christ is alive!*

Listen to the words of Napoleon Bonaparte after he was exiled. As he contemplated his exploits in Europe versus the legacy of Jesus, he came to this stunning conclusion:

> I know men, and I tell you that Jesus Christ is no mere man. Between Him and every other person in the world, there is no possible term of comparison. Alexander, Caesar, Charlemagne, and myself founded great empires; but upon what did the creations of our genius depend? Upon force. Jesus alone founded His empire upon love, and to this very day millions would die for Him.[3]

THE DECISION YOU MUST MAKE

In the end the decision about Jesus Christ must become very personal. Who do *you* think he is? Is He the Son of God? Is He the Messiah from heaven? Is He a misunderstood Palestinian rabbi? Is He who He claimed to be? Or is He something else altogether?

May I submit to you that when all the alternatives are fairly considered, we are left with only three options concerning Jesus Christ.

1. *He might be a liar.* Perhaps He wasn't telling the truth at all. If so, then He falls into the category of those religious charlatans who come along from time to time selling spiritual snake oil to the gullible. But note this: If Jesus is a liar, then He is the biggest and most successful liar in history since over two billion people have followed His lies.

2. *He might be a lunatic.* Let us suppose that you desire a more charitable judgment on Jesus. Is it possible that He was well-meaning but deluded? Could it be that He thought He was telling the truth, but like those poor souls who think they are Napoleon, He deserved to be locked away in an asylum? Is that your judgment on Jesus? If so, the question remains, how could so many evidently normal people follow a madman for so many centuries? Lunatics gain a following for a time but are eventually found out. How has this madman from Galilee continued to trick people after twenty centuries?

3. *He might be the Lord.* If the first two alternatives don't suit you, perhaps you will consider this one (it really is the only option left): A man who said the things Jesus said was either a liar or a lunatic or He was (and is) the Lord from heaven. And if He is the Lord from heaven, you dare not remain neutral. You must give account for

how you respond. If He is the Lord, you must yield your life to Him. No other response will suffice.

C. S. LEWIS ON JESUS

Does this scenario seem unfair to you, as if perhaps the deck has been stacked to force you to a predetermined conclusion? It is possible that you wish to consider a fourth alternative, one that is popular with many people. It is sometimes said this way: "When I look at Jesus, I see the greatest moral teacher the world has ever known. He may or may not be the Son of God—to me that doesn't matter— what's important is that I recognize and follow His moral teachings." Is such a view compatible with the New Testament picture of Jesus Christ? Does it present Him as a great moral teacher or as the ultimate example for mankind? We have already discussed this view somewhat, but we need to take a closer look at it now.

In his book *Mere Christianity*, C. S. Lewis considers this very common viewpoint and concludes his chapter "The Shocking Alternative" with these penetrating words:

> I am trying here to prevent anyone saying the really foolish thing that people often say about Him: "I'm ready to accept Jesus as a great moral teacher, but I don't accept His claim to be God." That is the one thing we must not say. A man who was merely a man and said the sort of things Jesus said would not be a great moral teacher. He would either be a lunatic—on a level with the man who says he is a poached egg—or else he would be the devil of Hell. You must make your choice. Either this man was, and is, the Son of God; or else a madman or something worse. You can shut Him up for a fool, you can spit

at Him or kill Him as a demon; or you can fall at His feet and call Him Lord and God. But let us not come with any patronizing nonsense about His being a great human teacher. He has not left that open to us. He did not intend to.[4]

We've come now to the very end of this chapter. If you are still unsure about Jesus, let me encourage you to pick up the New Testament and read it for yourself. You don't have to take my word for any of this. If what I am saying is true, the facts ought to be self-evident to any intelligent man or woman. Please don't make a final decision about Jesus without checking things out for yourself. Pick any one of the four Gospels—Matthew, Mark, Luke, or John—and read the story of Jesus for yourself. Make notes. Ask questions as you read. Think about this amazing man who walked on Planet Earth twenty centuries ago. Who was He? Who is He? What do *you* say?

THE BOTTOM LINE

I close by placing before you the three great alternatives regarding Jesus: *He's a liar, He's a lunatic, or He's the Lord.* Two thousand years ago Jesus asked His disciples to answer one all-important question: "Who do you say I am?" (Matthew 16:15).

Listed below are three alternatives regarding Jesus. I'm going to ask you to check the *yes* blank next to the one you believe is correct, then sign your name beneath and fill in the date.

I've told you what I believe and what Christians everywhere believe about Jesus. But you can't get to heaven on someone else's faith. It's time to sign on the bottom line for yourself.

I say Jesus was the Son of God who came to be my Savior, and I am trusting Him with all my heart. What do *you* say?

He's a liar.	_____	Yes	_____	No
He's a lunatic.	_____	Yes	_____	No
He's the Lord.	_____	Yes	_____	No
Signed _____				
Date _____				

If you're still not sure about Jesus, may I ask you to reread this chapter one more time, noting every Bible verse I mention. Before you render your final verdict, please take the time to check each verse for yourself. Study the evidence on your own. Then make up your mind about Jesus Christ.

SOMETHING TO THINK ABOUT

The fact of Christ is an unanswerable argument. He *must* be accounted for and He cannot be accounted for on the theory that He was merely a man.

—WILLIAM JENNINGS BRYAN

QUESTIONS TO CONSIDER

1. How do you account for the continuing popularity of Jesus Christ?

2. Define Mt. Rushmore religion. What's wrong with it?

3. How would unbelievers answer the claims of Christ as presented in this chapter?

4. Why is it impossible to believe that Jesus was only a good teacher or a good man and nothing more?

5. Do you believe that Jesus rose from the dead? Why or why not?

6. If someone were to ask you, "Do you have a personal relationship with Jesus Christ?" how would you answer that question?

SCRIPTURES TO PONDER

John 10:1-30

Philippians 2:5-11

Revelation 5

Four

THE GOD
WE HARDLY KNOW

What a Christian Believes
About the Holy Spirit

Television host David Mains caught me off guard with his question. "If you had to grade your congregation on their knowledge of the Holy Spirit, what grade would you give them?"

Up until that question, the interview had gone well. David and his daughter Melissa had thrown me fast pitches right over the center of the plate, and I had proceeded to knock the ball out of the park each time.

Suddenly I was at a loss for words. But the one thing you can't do on TV is say nothing. The camera hates dead airtime. So I blurted out my answer: "I would give my congregation a C+ on the knowledge of the Holy Spirit." It seemed a safe grade to me—not too high, not too low. But evidently I sounded like the proverbial hard-nosed teacher because David looked at me with a frown.

Now I was really in trouble. It sounded like I was putting down my own church. So I quickly said something like, "Look, if you graded my congregation on their knowledge of God the Father, I would give them an A, and on Jesus Christ, I would give them an A+. But I don't think we know as much about the Holy Spirit as we do about the Father and the Son."

David Mains smiled and said, "That's fair," so I knew I was off the hook. Sort of.

ALWAYS THE FIRST QUESTION

Whenever I am interviewed on this subject, the first question is almost always the same: "Why don't we know more about the Holy Spirit?"

God the Father—we know about Him.

God the Son—we know Him even better.

But the Holy Spirit? That's another story. He's the God we hardly know.

Acts 19 records the story of Paul's first visit to Ephesus, where he met some disciples of John the Baptist. When Paul asked if they had received the Holy Spirit when they believed, they replied with total honesty, "No, we have not even heard that there is a Holy Spirit" (verse 2). Many contemporary Christians could say virtually the same thing.

Oh, we know about the Trinity, even if we can't explain the doctrine. But most of us would be hard-pressed to pass a midterm exam on the person and work of the Holy Spirit.

So what grade would you give yourself in terms of your personal knowledge of the Holy Spirit?

I'd like to give you a short cram course on the biblical doctrine of the Holy Spirit. It's impossible for me to cover the entire range of truth about the Holy Spirit in just one chapter, but I think I can help you come to a basic grasp of who He is, what He does, and how you can receive His power in your life.

WHO IS THE HOLY SPIRIT?

Any investigation of the Holy Spirit must begin with this fundamental question. A great deal of our confusion stems from the fact that we don't know the right answer.

There are two fundamental facts about the Spirit that you need to know.

The Holy Spirit Is a Person

This may seem obvious to you, but it isn't obvious to everyone. Some people speak of the Holy Spirit as an impersonal power or influence. They speak of the Holy Spirit as an "it." If you saw the *Star Wars* movies, you'll remember the phrase, "May the Force be with you." That's how many people think of the Spirit—as a mysterious force from heaven that somehow helps us on earth.

But the Bible clearly refers to the Holy Spirit in terms that can only apply to a person. For instance, the Holy Spirit possesses a mind (Romans 8:27), He speaks (Acts 13:2), He gives commands (Acts 8:29), and He has a will (1 Corinthians 12:11). Ephesians 4:30 says, "Do not grieve the Holy Spirit." But you can't grieve a force or a power. You can only grieve another person.

In John 16:13 Jesus says of the Holy Spirit, "He will speak only what he hears, and he will tell you what is yet to come." That passage is important because Jesus clearly calls the Holy Spirit a "he."

All the attributes of personality are given to the Holy Spirit in the New Testament. Therefore, we may say that the Holy Spirit is a person, not a mere force or an impersonal power.

The Holy Spirit Is God

The second truth is that the Holy Spirit is not only a person, He is a divine person. *That is to say, He is God.* In the famous story of Ananias and Sapphira in Acts 5, Peter says in verse 3 that they had sinned against the Holy Spirit, but in verse 4 he says they had sinned against God. Which is correct? Both, because the Holy Spirit is God. That's why when Jesus gave the Great Commission (Matthew 28:19-20), He commanded the disciples to baptize "in the name of the Father and of the Son and of the Holy Spirit." One name, three persons. That's the doctrine of the Trinity clearly stated. The Father is God, the Son is God, and the Holy Spirit is God.

Most of us have trouble understanding this doctrine, and we have even more difficulty explaining it to a friend. I heard Tony Evans say, "Give 'em a pretzel." A pretzel is one piece of dough twisted and baked so that it contains three holes. Each hole is part of the pretzel, but the holes are different from each other. One pretzel, three parts. Not a perfect illustration but not bad!

Now if you put these two truths together, what do you get? Since the Holy Spirit is a person, you can have a personal relationship with Him. And since He is God, His power is God's power. Therefore, in relating to the Holy Spirit, you are coming into personal contact with the God of the universe.

It is through the Holy Spirit that God enters the human heart and changes it for the better. What a tremendous truth this is. And how unfortunate that few Christians understand how the Holy Spirit can change their lives.

WHAT DOES HE DO?

Theologians often divide the work of the Trinity this way:

- God the Father is the *source* of all things.
- God the Son is the *channel* of all things.
- God the Spirit is the *agent* of all things.

Regarding the source, all things flow from the Father's will. Regarding the channel, all of God's blessing flow to us through Jesus Christ the Son. But it is the Holy Spirit who acts as the agent of the Almighty, and He carries out the directives of the Father.

In History

I've been amazed to discover that the Holy Spirit is everywhere in the Bible. The first mention is in Genesis 1:2, and the last mention of the Spirit is in Revelation 22:17. He's present at the moment of creation, and He's there at the very end of the Bible. In the Old Testament you see the Holy Spirit coming with great power upon kings, priests, judges (deliverers), and military leaders. He is also the one who inspired the poets to sing and gave the prophets a message to proclaim. He is the cloud by day and the fiery pillar by night that led Israel through the wilderness. He was the one who lifted Ezekiel when the people were in captivity. He was also the one who enabled Zerubbabel to rebuild the temple.

When you come to the New Testament, you especially see Him at work in the life of Christ. Our Lord was conceived by the Holy Spirit, and the Spirit came upon Him at His baptism, led Him into the wilderness, filled Him with power to work miracles, bore witness that He was the Son of God, was with Him at the crucifixion, and raised Him from the dead. All that Jesus did, He did in the power of the Holy Spirit. "God anointed Jesus of Nazareth with the Holy Spirit and power, and . . . he went around doing good and healing all who were under the power of the devil, because God was with him" (Acts 10:38).

The Holy Spirit was there at Pentecost when the church was born. He was there when Peter and Paul preached all across the Roman Empire. It was the Holy Spirit who gave the apostles boldness to preach in the face of persecution and indifference. It was the Holy Spirit who brought unity to the early church and caused it to grow in spite of fierce opposition.

Everywhere you turn in the Bible, you see the Holy Spirit at work. *He is the unseen hand of God moving through human history to accomplish God's purposes on the earth.*

In the World Today

But what is the Holy Spirit doing on earth today? We can answer that from the words of Jesus in John 16:8: "When he [the Holy Spirit] comes, he will convict the world of guilt in regard to sin and righteousness and judgment." The word translated "convict" comes from the drama of a courtroom trial. It refers to what the prosecuting attorney does when he argues his case. He puts the defendant on the witness stand and begins to pile up the evidence. Fact upon fact, witness upon witness, truth upon truth, slowly, inexorably, irresistibly building his case until finally the enormity of the evidence is so overwhelming that the judge is forced to say to the defendant, "I find you guilty beyond a reasonable doubt." Furthermore, this word means to present the evidence in such an overwhelming fashion that even the defendant is compelled at the end of the trial to step up and say, "I admit it. I confess. I am guilty."

These words of Jesus are literally true today. The Holy Spirit works through us so that as we share the Gospel with men and women, they are convicted of their true moral guilt before God. As we share the Gospel they come to the conclusion, "Yes, I am guilty. Yes, I need a Savior—I need Jesus Christ."

In Believers

What does the Holy Spirit do for those who have received Jesus Christ as their own Savior? Here are just some of the things He does:

- He baptizes believers into the Body of Christ, the universal church (1 Corinthians 12:13).
- He seals all believers, thus assuring them of their salvation (Ephesians 1:13).
- He indwells every believer with His personal presence (1 Corinthians 6:19-20)
- He gives spiritual gifts to every believer (1 Corinthians 12:1, 11).
- He produces the fruit of a godly life in us (Galatians 5:22-23).
- He enables us to put to death the deeds of the flesh (Romans 8:13).
- He prays for us when we can't pray for ourselves (Romans 8:26-27).
- He spreads the love of God in our hearts (Romans 5:5).

- He enables us to triumph in the midst of suffering (1 Peter 4:19).
- He empowers us to boldly witness for Christ (Acts 1:8).
- He makes the things of God real to us (1 Corinthians 2:10-14).
- He fills us so that we can please God every day (Ephesians 5:18).
- He creates unity between believers (Ephesians 4:3).
- He guarantees our final salvation in heaven (Ephesians 1:14).

In short, the Holy Spirit does everything needed to bring us to Christ, everything we need to walk with Christ in this life, and everything needed to take us safely from earth to heaven. He does it all for us, and He does it for all of us. *None of us could live even one day as a Christian without the aid of the Holy Spirit.*[1]

HOW CAN WE RECEIVE HIS BLESSING?

Only one question remains: *How can we receive the blessing of the Holy Spirit?* Everything up until this point has dealt with theology in the abstract, but our greatest need is to know the Spirit deeply and personally. It's never enough to possess the truth; the truth must eventually possess us in order to change us.

The Command—Be Continually Filled

Ephesians 5:18 says, "Be filled with the Spirit." In the Greek that phrase is a present passive imperative. An imperative is a command—"Be *filled*." The passive voice means that we are not commanded to fill ourselves but rather to *be* filled with the Holy Spirit.

And the present tense describes something that happens continually. You could legitimately translate this verse "Be continually filled with the Holy Spirit."

God's desire—and His command—for you and me is that we should be continually filled with the Holy Spirit. That means that the filling of the Spirit is not a one-time affair that happens in a crisis but is meant to be the normal ongoing experience of every Christian.

The Need for Renewal

We need the continual filling of the Spirit because we are leaky vessels. As each day wears on, as the pressures of life ebb and flow, we may find ourselves depending less on the Holy Spirit and more on our own resources to get ourselves out of trouble or to handle the crises of life. And so we become bossy or petty or unkind or impatient or just plain cranky and hard to live with. We say mean things to people we love, we fly off the handle, or we get silent and refuse to speak to others.

That's why we need to come to the Lord many times each day, asking for a new and fresh infilling of the Spirit. We need new power, new blessing, new strength to face the challenges of the day.

But how do we receive this?

Bill Bright's Suggestion

In one of his books D. James Kennedy shares something that Bill Bright said to Kennedy's congregation (the Coral Ridge Presbyterian Church in Fort Lauderdale, Florida) a few years ago.[2] Bright told them that unconfessed sin grieves the Holy Spirit, and therefore they could never experience His blessing until they dealt with the sin in their lives. What I am going to share with you is what Dr. Bright said that day. The first step is to be totally honest with the Lord about your spiritual condition. Begin with the sins of the flesh (what you were before coming to Christ)—anger, bitterness, wrath, malice, unkindness, drunkenness, immorality, impurity, gossip, slander, greed, pride, sloth, gluttony, envy, lust. Take a piece of paper and note the sins the Lord brings to mind. Just write them down, listing each one. Then sit in silence for a period of time, asking God to show you anything else that displeases Him. Whatever the Lord shows you, write it down.

At this point, wait in silence a second time, relying on the prayer of David in Psalm 19:12, "Who can discern his errors? Forgive my hidden faults." As you wait, ask God to turn the searchlight of His truth upon your soul. It will take courage to do this, but God always answers the sincere prayer of a penitent child of God. You *will* get a special delivery message from God. Whatever else God shows you, write it down.

Eventually you will come to the place where you are free of offense to both God and man. For the first time in your life, you will be able to pray with a clear conscience. Now take the sheet of paper and write over it, "The blood of Jesus, his Son, purifies us from every sin" (1 John 1:7). Then take the paper and destroy it.

86 Sins!

Bill Bright's counsel gripped my soul. So I got up early one Sunday morning and went to the church determined to follow his advice.

As I sat at my desk, I pulled out a sheet of white paper and began to write down my sins, faults, and shortcomings, listing every area of life that I knew to be displeasing to the Lord. In order to help me think about specific sins, I referred to some of the lists in the New Testament that mention either sins or the moral standards God desires from His children. Some of those passages are Romans 1:24-32, Galatians 5:15-23, Ephesians 4:25—5:8, Philippians 2:1-4, 4:5-8, Colossians 3:1-14, 1 Timothy 3:1-7, and Titus 2:11-14. One could also look at the Ten Commandments (Exodus 20:1-17) in this regard.

I decided to open my heart before the Lord and write down everything He brought to mind. My pen flew across the paper as the Lord showed me many things in my life that displeased Him. Some were sins of omission, things I should have done that I neglected to do. Others were wrong attitudes, hasty words, a tendency toward thoughtless chatter, and a streak of unkindness toward those I love the most.

Someone may ask if such a moral inventory is healthy. Could this not make a person too introspective? My answer is, it depends. I would not recommend doing such soul-searching every day. But from time to time it's good to stop and do some deep cleaning of the soul.

Within thirty minutes I had filled an entire page. I discovered that I had written down eighty-six specific areas of my life that needed change. As I studied the list, I found that these were not eighty-six independent sins; rather, many were variations on a theme, most of them related in one way or another to the classic seven deadly sins of pride, greed, sloth, gluttony, envy, anger, and lust.

It wasn't a pretty list, but I didn't feel depressed when I read it.

Instead, I felt liberated and almost exhilarated, as if an enormous load had been lifted from my shoulders.

So this is the truth about Ray Pritchard?

Indeed it is. I say with the saints of all ages that in me—that is, in my flesh—dwells not a single good thing. Apart from the grace of God at work in my life, I am a sinner lost and undone. My life, like Jeremiah's, is deceitful and wicked (Jeremiah 17:9). I do not know the half of my sinfulness.

When the list was complete, I wrote across it in big red letters the word FORGIVEN! Underneath I wrote out 1 John 1:7. After sharing this story with my congregation, I destroyed the list that afternoon without showing it to anyone else.

But having done that exercise, I found it very easy to pray for the filling of the Holy Spirit. I also found it easy to believe that God answered my prayer.

If you have never made such a moral inventory of your life, I encourage you to do so as soon as you finish reading this chapter.

CHRIST AT HOME IN YOUR HEART

Think of your heart—your life—as a house with many rooms. All of us have special rooms in our homes that we reserve for entertaining our guests. Most of us also have closets, basements, and attics that we try to keep out of public view because they are messy or contain items we don't want others to see. The same is true in the spiritual realm. Many of us have welcomed Christ into a large part of our hearts, but there are other areas of our lives where He is not welcome. It might be our soul's kitchen or bedroom or recreation room that we keep locked from public view. Usually there is some hidden sin—anger or bitterness or greed or lust or theft or jealousy or promiscuous behavior—of which we are ashamed. Perhaps we don't want Him to rearrange those parts of our lives. Perhaps we like things as they are. But we will never be happy and Christ will never be fully at home until every door is opened to Him.[3]

If you want to know the power of the Spirit, the price is simple but not easy to pay. *You must open those hidden doors and allow the Lord Jesus to come in and make all things new.* Will it be painful? Perhaps. But the hardest part is opening the doors one by one. If you have the courage to let Christ into every room of your life, He will come in and redecorate your life so it is more beautiful than you ever imagined possible.

But you'll never know until you start opening those doors.

SOMETHING TO THINK ABOUT

Every time we say, "I believe in the Holy Spirit," we mean that we believe that there is a living God able and willing to enter human personality and change it.

—J. B. PHILLIPS

QUESTIONS TO CONSIDER

1. Why don't we know more about the Holy Spirit? What grade would you give yourself in this area? What happens to a church when the truth about the Holy Spirit is ignored or downplayed?

2. Why is it important to know that the Holy Spirit is a person and not an impersonal force or power?

3. What role does the Holy Spirit play in evangelism? How should His work affect the way we share Christ with others?

4. Which ministries of the Holy Spirit seem most important in your own life?

5. Are you filled with the Spirit? If you aren't sure, what needs to happen before you can answer yes?

6. Take time to do a room by room inventory of your heart. Invite Christ to make Himself at home and to redecorate your life any way He chooses.

SCRIPTURES TO PONDER

Romans 8:1-17
Galatians 5:22-23
Ephesians 4:29-32

Five

IN THE BEGINNING

What a Christian Believes About Creation

> *In the beginning God created the heavens and the earth.*
> —GENESIS 1:1

First sentences matter. Every writer knows that the very first words he puts on paper set the tone for everything that follows. In fact, most writers work for hours trying to come up with just the right combination of words that will properly introduce their subject and then entice the reader to keep reading. There are very few rules for good first sentences. They may be short or long, complex or simple, descriptive or declarative, but above all else, a good first sentence invites the reader into the book with a promise of good things to follow.

The Bible begins with a wonderful first sentence. In fact, it is one of the greatest first sentences in all of literature. It contains only ten words in English and seven in Hebrew. Seven of the ten English words contain one syllable, two contain two syllables, and one contains three syllables. None of the words are difficult, ornate, or unusual in any way. There are no subordinate clauses, no pronouns, and only one preposition. I daresay you would be hard-pressed to write a simpler sentence yourself.

Genesis 1:1 is entirely straightforward and easy to understand. This is where the Bible begins, and in truth this is where *everything* begins. You may recall the famous scene from *The Sound of Music* when Julie Andrews (playing Maria) is trying to teach the children to sing. "Let's start at the very beginning," she says, "That's a very good place to start."

Indeed it is. In this chapter we have before us the very beginning of the Bible. This is the first sentence of the first chapter of the first book of the Holy Scriptures. Everything that will follow flows from this declaration.

This is the first great truth God wants us to know. Know this, and the universe makes sense. Doubt this or deny this or ignore this, and you have missed the central reality of life.

Genesis 1:1 is sublime in its simplicity. It is at one and the same time majestic, overpowering, and mysterious. It is also complete in itself. Here we have moved far beyond the battlefield of science to a realm the laboratory can never touch.

HE CAN MAKE A DONKEY TALK

I call your attention to the setting of this verse. It tells us in a simple declarative fashion how everything that is, came into being. It is the divine answer to the question, "Where did all this come from?" Everything that exists in heaven and on earth, everything that might be found in the farthest reaches of the most remote galaxies, and all that might be discovered in the most minute particles of the subatomic region—all of it comes from God, and all of it belongs to God, because He created all that is and was and ever will be.

I think it is useful to point out that the Bible begins with a declaration, not with an argument. God never bothers trying to prove His existence. Better a giant should prove himself to an earthworm than that Almighty God should prove Himself to us. Furthermore, there is no explanation given for why God created the universe. For that matter, there is no definition of God. In the words of Sergeant Joe Friday of *Dragnet*, "Just the facts, ma'am, just the facts." Genesis 1:1 brings us face to face with ultimate truth: "In the beginning God created the heavens and the earth."

I said earlier that everything in the Bible flows from this truth. There's another way of saying that. *If you can accept Genesis 1:1, you won't have any trouble with the rest of the Bible.* People who have trouble accepting the miracles of the Bible almost always doubt the truth of Genesis as well. But if God created everything—and if He did it by His own powerful word—if He spoke and everything came into being—if that's true, then why should we doubt that He can also work miracles? If He can make the rules, He can suspend them or change them anytime He wants to. If He can speak and call forth the stars in the sky, certainly He can cause one of those stars to lead the wise men to Bethlehem. If He can create a furry donkey, He can make that donkey talk. If He can cause a virgin to conceive and give birth to the Son of God, He can also raise His Son from the dead.

Miracles are no problem for those who truly believe the first verse of the Bible. But for those who doubt the first verse, everything in the Bible will be a struggle. Therefore, I urge you to rest your faith on the firm foundation of the very first verse of the Bible. If you can believe that, you can believe everything else you read in the Bible.

With that as a background, let's think together about the following question: If Genesis 1:1 is true, then what other things must also be true and what things cannot be true? We'll start with the negative.

WHAT CANNOT BE TRUE

First of all, if Genesis 1:1 is true, then *atheism is impossible*, for our text clearly states, "In the beginning *God* created." Here is a fundamental fact, or axiom if you will, of the spiritual life. There is a God who created all things. But some people refuse to believe in God. They flatly deny His existence. Such people have existed in every age. But we must recognize this: Atheism is not a philosophy but a religious statement. It is also a denial of reality. *It is the supreme folly because it ignores the central reality of the universe.* It disregards God and degrades man to the level of a mere brute. It is also the most unnatural philosophy in the world. No one is born an atheist. We are all born with an inner awareness of a Higher Power (see Romans 1:18-21), and even though we suppress that truth through sin, the divine imprint remains within us.

Since atheism is unnatural, it is a hard position to hold. Since every flower testifies to God and every star proclaims His power, one must be willfully blind to the evidence to maintain his or her atheism. That's why Psalm 14:1 tells us that only a "fool" would say, "There is no God."

Second, if Genesis 1:1 is true, *materialism is not true*. Materialism is the philosophy that declares that matter is eternal and has always existed. But the Bible says, "In the beginning." That means the universe had a birthday.

Third, if Genesis 1:1 is true, *polytheism is not true.* Polytheism means "many gods," but Genesis 1:1 declares that the universe was created by God and God alone. This must have come as a shock to the nations surrounding Israel in the time of Moses—the Hivites, the Girgashites, the Canaanites, the Hittites, and later the Moabites, the Philistines, and still later the Assyrians and the Babylonians. In one simple sentence the foundation is removed from every pagan religion.

Fourth, if Genesis 1:1 is true, *humanism is not true.* Humanism declares that man is the center of all things and the measure of all things. It is the polluted fountain from which we get situation ethics, relativism, and the postmodern denial of absolute truth. But the Bible tells us that God—not man—created all things. Almighty God stands at the center of the universe, and all creation must answer to Him.

Fifth, if Genesis 1:1 is true, *fatalism cannot be true.* This philosophy suggests that there is no intelligent being who guides all things and that we are here strictly by chance. We come from nowhere, we have no reason to be here, and we are going nowhere in particular when we die. But the Bible declares that God created us, and if God created us, then we have a purpose—to live for His glory.

Sixth, if Genesis 1:1 is true, *pantheism cannot be true.* Pantheism is the root philosophy of all Eastern religions and of the New Age movement. It suggests that the universe is simply an extension of some great cosmic power. All things are part of God, and God is part of all things. But to the contrary, God *created* the heavens and the earth. He created them, and He inhabits them, but He is not the universe, and the universe is not God.

Seventh, if Genesis 1:1 is true, *then evolution cannot possibly be true.* Here I speak not of change and variation within species and the biblical kinds, which we may all see with our eyes (such as changes to peppered moths and fruit flies and the development of new varieties of dogs through selective breeding). I am referring to naturalistic evolution—the theory that the universe came into being billions of years ago through a purposeless, undirected, random act, and that all things have slowly evolved over the aeons from the simpler to the more complex, including all life forms on earth and including man himself.[1] Such a viewpoint is flatly ruled out by the very first verse of the Bible. Instead of the impersonal hand of evolution with its unending ages of time, chance, struggle, and death, we have the simple and majestic statement that God created all things.

Let us not be coy about what this really means. *Evolution as a worldview is diametrically opposed to biblical faith.* It is pagan at its root and evil in its fruit.

Here, then, are seven prevalent philosophies that fail the test of the very first verse of the Bible. It is an impressive list: Atheism, materialism, polytheism, humanism, fatalism, pantheism, and evolution. Millions of people—no, hundreds of millions of people, perhaps billions of people—around the world have followed these empty philosophies to their eternal loss. They could have been saved from their error if only they had considered Genesis 1:1.

WHAT MUST BE TRUE

We will now consider the other side of the coin. What things must be true if Genesis 1:1 is true?

First, if this verse is true, *the God of the Bible must be truly awesome.* If we had only Genesis 1:1 and nothing else, we would know that God is all-powerful, all-wise, a God of enormous creativity and variety, a God of purposeful action, a God of sovereign authority. We know that He must be eternal, for nothing can never bring forth something. He must always have existed. He must be beyond the limits of time and space because He created time and space; they would not exist without Him. We would also infer from creation that His purposes are good and not evil because He created the universe to bring glory to Himself.[2]

Second, if this verse is true, *science can never give us final answers to the most important questions of life.* Science can tell us many things, but it cannot tell us everything we would like to know about where we came from, who created us, how we got here, or precisely what methods God used to create the universe. Some things are simply hidden in the mind and counsel of God. This means that after all our arguing and debating is over, there will still be many things we simply don't understand. I say that because Genesis 1:1 takes us beyond the seen to the unseen. It transports us from the material to the spiritual, from the passing to the permanent, from the temporal to the eternal, from the natural to the supernatural. It moves into a realm where science simply cannot go.

This truth humbles all of us because it means we must look to God for the answers to the ultimate questions of life. Hebrews 11:3 tells us that faith in God is a prerequisite to properly understanding questions of ultimate origin: "By faith we understand that the universe was formed at God's command, so that what is seen was not made out of what was visible." Theologians have a word for this. They call it *cre-*

ation ex nihilo, which means "creation out of nothing." God spoke, and the universe came into being. That's why Genesis 1 repeats the phrase, "and God said . . . and God said . . . and God said." God spoke, and the continents formed. He spoke, and the stars took their places in the heavens. He spoke, and the fish began to swim. He spoke, and the birds began to fly. He spoke, and the coyote began to howl. He spoke, and the lion roared. Finally, He spoke, and Adam came into being. And when Adam went to sleep, God took a rib and fashioned Eve.

That's how God does things. When He wants to create something, He speaks and it happens. When He wants a giraffe, He says, "Giraffe, come to life," and there's a giraffe! He says, "Let there be a universe," and a universe exists where none existed before. It's like the slogan we see on Christian T-shirts: "I believe in the Big Bang Theory. God said it, and Bang! It happened."

When God created the universe, He didn't use preexisting materials, and He didn't create piecemeal. He spoke, and the universe came into being in exactly the manner recorded in Genesis 1.

Third, if Genesis 1:1 is true, *we don't need the help of naturalistic evolution to understand the universe around us.* By making that statement, I don't mean to imply that the Bible tells us everything we would like to know about the universe. It is often said that the Bible is not a textbook on science. That is a dangerous half-truth because it can lead us to a two-compartment theory of life, in which we put our faith on one shelf and our science on the other and never mix the two. While it is true that the Bible is not a textbook on science, I would argue that it is literally true in all its details—and that includes the details in Genesis.

Many Christians secretly believe that the Bible and science are mortal enemies. But that's not true. Science rightly understood is the Christian's friend. The only conflict comes when we take the unproven theories of science—such as naturalistic evolution—and use them as our starting point for interpreting the Bible. That always leads us away from truth and ultimately away from God.

While recognizing the many great discoveries of modern science, we refuse to give secular scientists the final word on how the universe came to be and how human life developed on earth. Francis Schaeffer stated it well when he said that when all the facts are finally in, we will discover that there is no final conflict between the Bible rightly interpreted and the facts of science rightly understood.[3]

Fourth, if Genesis 1:1 is true, *any attempt to understand the universe apart from God is doomed to fail.* Proverbs 1:7 reminds us that "the fear of the LORD is the beginning of knowledge." When you leave God out of education, then what you have is a system that produces intellectual giants and moral pygmies. When you leave God out of government, what you get is leaders without character. When you leave God out of public debate, you get a moral crisis in the White House and condoms in the high schools. When you leave God out of families, you get broken homes and latchkey kids. When you leave God out of science, you get naturalistic evolution.

Because Genesis 1:1 is true, we must say clearly that nothing makes sense in the universe if we leave God out. The Bible begins by putting God at the center of everything. To say it another way, He is Number One, and there is no number two.

Fifth, if Genesis 1:1 is true, *all our debating about creation and evolution should begin with the question, "What does the Bible say?"* I think this is where so many Christians get into trouble. Having been brain-

washed into believing that evolution must be true, they feel intimi-
dated by those who say the universe must be billions and billions of
years old and that God created life on earth through a process of slow
development over millions and millions of years. I would suggest
that a straightforward reading of the biblical text does not lead you
in that direction. While vast ages for the universe aren't necessarily
ruled out by Genesis 1—11, they aren't required by the text either.

I know there's great debate these days over the age of the earth.
If you ask me how old the earth is, I'd say I don't know because the
Bible doesn't give us a precise date. I do believe there is room for
reasonable discussion on this issue. However, I don't think the
world is necessarily as old as some people say it is. God could easily have created the whole world a few thousand years ago if He
wanted to do it that way. He could have created a mature universe,
fully functioning, from the very first moment. There is absolutely
no problem with that concept.

It seems most natural to me to understand the "days" of Genesis
1 as literal twenty-four hour days and that the most natural reading of the text is to understand it as teaching a recent creation of the
earth in six twenty-four hour days.

Could God have done it in millions and billions of years?
Absolutely. He's God, and He can do what he wants. Please think
carefully about the next sentence. *Christians who believe the Bible can
have as much time or as little as they need for God to create the universe.*
If you think God created the universe ten billion years ago, you can
say that because God could have done it that way. And I can say
He did it a few thousand years ago because that's no problem for
God either. But the evolutionist has no choice. He *must* have mil-

lions and billions of years. By leaving God out of the picture, the evolutionist has nothing left but time, chance, struggle, and death. In fact, for the naturalistic evolutionist, time becomes his God. He's forced to believe that anything is possible given enough time. That's why the evolutionist can give up anything except the time issue. He *has* to have millions and billions of years or else his theory (which is really his religion) falls to the ground.

My point is, we Christians don't need millions and billions of years in the universe. We can have it if we want it, but we don't need it. We have a God who can do whatever He wants whenever He wants to. The evolutionist worships at the altar of time because that's his only hope.

Sixth, if Genesis 1:1 is true, *we Christians should stand our ground with a cheerful spirit.* Sometimes we tend to get agitated over these things, and sometimes we like to argue among ourselves. Sometimes we get angry at the evolutionary brainwashing that goes on in the larger culture. But I am reminded of what one of my theology professors used to say. He told us not to get angry because when you leave God out, evolution is the best you can do. I think he's right.

NOT FREE TO PICK AND CHOOSE

"In the beginning God created the heavens and the earth." You either believe that or you don't. If you doubt it, you can't believe anything else in the Bible. If you believe it, you can believe anything else the Bible says.

We are not free to pick and choose which parts of the Bible we want to believe. You can't say, "I'll start at Psalm 23 because it touches my soul." The Lord who is the divine shepherd of Psalm 23 is the God who created the heavens and the earth in Genesis 1:1. By the same token, you can't decide to accept John 3:16 without also accepting Genesis 1:1 because the God who so loved the world is the same God who created it in the first place.[4]

Some people say it's hard to believe God created the world. *To the contrary, it is the easiest thing in the world to believe it.* Just open your eyes and look around. Do you believe the world in all its beauty, order, and complexity happened by chance? Do you believe the stars simply happened to evolve over billions of years?

The truth is, knowledge about God comes to us naturally, from Him. That's why little children aren't atheists. We're born with the knowledge of God implanted in us. Adults have to work hard to become atheists and evolutionists.

Light from God streams in on every side. You have to shut your eyes to keep from seeing it.

THREE GREAT QUESTIONS

But that leads to one final point: *Since the universe as it is rests on God's Word, no one can understand the universe properly without a knowledge of God.* If you leave God out, you've missed the fundamental truth about the universe. That means that in order to understand human origins and the true history of the universe, you must begin with God's understanding as He has revealed it to us in His Word. Start there and you start on firm ground. Start anywhere else and you sink into the quicksand of humanistic unbelief.

No one can know the universe and the answers to the great

questions of life without also knowing God. There are three great questions of life:

- Where did I come from?
- Why am I here?
- Where am I going?

The first question is the most fundamental. Until you answer it, you cannot answer the last two properly. If you think you evolved up from the slime, if you believe you arrived on the earth by chance as the result of blind evolution over millions and billions of years, if you believe you are the product of an evolutionary stream that started when a bolt of lightning hit the primordial soup in the dim reaches of the distant past, if that is what you believe about yourself, then you don't truly know where you came from or why you are here or where you are going.

Genesis 1:1 gives us a firm foundation for our faith. It tells us that this universe had a definite beginning and that we are here by God's creation, not by some random mutation of purposeless evolution. Everything in the universe is here because God wanted it to be here. *And we ourselves—we are His stuff, the clay in His hands.* We belong to God, He made us the way we are, and we couldn't escape Him even if we tried. And we won't be happy until we know Him intimately. He put a God-shaped vacuum inside your heart that only He can fill. He made you, He loves you in spite of your sin, and He sent His Son to die on the cross and rise from the dead so you could go to heaven. Your Creator has become your Savior. That's how much God loves you.

The hymn writer said, "All things bright and beautiful, all creatures great and small, all things wise and wonderful, the Lord God made them all."[5] After listing many parts of God's creation, he summed up the truth in his final verse:

> *He gave us eyes to see them,*
> *And lips that we might tell,*
> *How great is God Almighty,*
> *Who has made all things well.*

Indeed He did. May the Lord gives us eyes to see what God has made and lips to tell of God our Creator and Jesus Christ His Son, our eternal Savior.

SOMETHING TO THINK ABOUT

The probability of life originating from accident is comparable to the probability of the unabridged dictionary resulting from an explosion in a print shop.

—EDWARD CONKLIN

QUESTIONS TO CONSIDER

1. "If you can accept Genesis 1:1, you won't have any trouble with the rest of the Bible." How do you feel about that statement? What does it really mean?

2. What negative consequences flow from denying that God created the heavens and the earth? Why is atheism a hard position to hold?

3. "God never bothers trying to prove His existence." Do you agree? If this is true, what does it suggest about the way we should present our views about God to others?

4. Why is evolution as a worldview fundamentally incompatible with biblical faith? How do you feel about attempts to combine evolution and the Christian faith?

5. Is what ways is science the Christian's friend? How can science become the Christian's enemy?

6. Please answer these three questions: Where did I come from? Why am I here? Where am I going?

SCRIPTURES TO PONDER

Genesis 1—2

Hebrews 11:3

2 Peter 3:3-7

Six

DID MICKEY MANTLE GO TO HEAVEN?

What a Christian Believes About the Forgiveness of Sins

Like many others of my generation, I can testify that I grew up with Mickey Mantle. Back then, in the late fifties and early sixties, he was one of the most famous sports figures in America. Schoolboys by the millions imitated his swing and dreamed of the day when they could make it to the big leagues and play baseball like "the Mick." *Sports Illustrated* called him "the last great player on the last great team."[1]

Mickey Mantle died in 1995 from deadly cancer that spread throughout his body. By his own admission, Mickey had abused his body through years of hard living and hard drinking. In the months before his death he liked to joke that when he got to the gates of heaven, the Lord would say, "Mickey, I can't let you in after the way you lived." As Mickey told the story, just as he turned to leave, the Lord would say, "But since you're here, would you mind signing six dozen baseballs for me?"

It's against that backdrop that I raise the question, did Mickey Mantle go to heaven? He was clearly thinking about heaven a lot in his last few days. He admitted he didn't deserve to go to heaven and expected the Lord to turn him away.

ENTER BOBBY RICHARDSON

During Mantle's funeral service in Dallas, former teammate Bobby Richardson told a packed sanctuary at the Lovers Lane Methodist Church how Mickey had called him and asked for prayer two days before he died. When he went to see him in the hospital that same day, Mickey told him, "I want you to know that I've accepted Jesus Christ as my Savior." Bobby Richardson wanted to make sure, so he shared the Gospel and explained what it meant to trust Christ as Savior. When he finished, Mickey Mantle said, "That's exactly what I did."[2] The next day, knowing that his death was near, Mickey said with a smile on his face, "I'm ready to go now. Let's get on with it." He died within a few hours.

Did Mickey Mantle go to heaven? To us the question may seem academic, but it was the most pressing question on his mind during those last few days in Dallas.

This chapter is not about heaven in general or even about salvation in general, but about the heart of salvation—the forgiveness of sin. This is the central truth of the Christian Gospel because no one can go to heaven unless his or her sins are forgiven.

"I BELIEVE IN THE FORGIVENESS OF SINS"

If you grew up in a liturgical church you probably recited the Apostles' Creed every Sunday. It begins with the words, "I believe in God the Father Almighty, maker of heaven and earth" and goes on to cover all the major Christian doctrines. Many scholars believe it goes back to the second century after Christ, meaning that it is perhaps the earliest surviving Christian creed. It's not very long, only two sentences that contain a number of short phrases. The second sentence goes like this: "I believe in the Holy Spirit, the holy catholic church, the communion of saints, the forgiveness of sins, the resurrection of the body, and the life everlasting. Amen."

Did you notice it? Tucked away in that list is the phrase "the forgiveness of sins." That strikes me as important because this ancient creed lists everything the early Christians considered essential to the Christian faith.

That's one reason I believe in the forgiveness of sins: Because the earliest Christians believed in it too. *They understood that at the heart of the Gospel is the message of forgiveness.*

THE NEED FOR FORGIVENESS

We need God's forgiveness because the Bible says we are lost in our sins. Isaiah 53:6 declares, "We all, like sheep, have gone astray, each of us has turned to his own way." Our problem is sin, and it is a problem that affects each of us. The famous words of Romans 3:23 remind us that "All have sinned and fall short of the glory of God." We need forgiveness because we are lost, and we are lost because we are sinners who have strayed away from God.

Talk Show Trash

Can anyone deny that America has strayed from God? If you doubt that, watch the daytime talk shows. They've gotten so bad that even the leaders in Washington think we need to do something about

them. Not long ago noted author William Bennett and several sen-
ators called for a voluntary curb on the smut being produced on TV
talk shows. If you don't believe me, here are some recent topics: husbands who cheated on their honeymoons, teenagers who murdered
their parents, men who date prostitutes, women pursuing the same
man, mothers of jilted daughters, people who have had one-night
stands, gay teenagers, and teens who object to their mothers' lovers.[3]

We Love This Stuff

Now before you say anything, ask yourself why this garbage is on
TV. It's there because people watch it. We wouldn't have shows like
this if viewers didn't want to see it. As a nation we love this stuff.
We eat it up; we watch it by the hour. We get vicarious pleasure out
of watching strange people parade their broken lives in front of a
national audience.

What do you think the major problem of America is? It's not the
debt limit or the budget crisis in Washington. It's not the race for the
White House. In fact, the major problem of America has nothing
whatsoever to do with politics.

Our problem is spiritual. *America is sick because we as a people are
sick.* We are truly like the lost sheep Isaiah talks about. Having gone
astray from God, we have trapped ourselves in the slime pit of
moral degradation.

- We're trapped, and we don't know it.
- We're lost, and we don't realize it.
- We're blind, and we don't know why we keep failing
  as a nation.

- We need forgiveness, but we don't know where
  to look for it.

Our sins have separated us from God. He is on one side, and we are on the other, and there is a great divide between us. We stand on one side and cry out, "Help! We need a bridge across this great divide." But who will build it for us?

THE PROVISION OF FORGIVENESS

God's answer to our need is wrapped up in a person. His name is Jesus. Acts 10:43 says, "All the prophets testify about him that everyone who believes in him receives forgiveness of sins through his name."

Someone may hear that and say, "Good! I believe in Jesus." But it's not enough to believe that Jesus existed or that He was a good man. It's not enough to believe *about* Jesus. The Bible says you must believe *in* Jesus in order to be saved.

On the Back of a Crucified Man

To be specific, you must trust in Jesus so much that if Jesus can't take you to heaven, you won't go there at all. Have you ever heard someone say, "Don't put all your eggs in one basket"? That may be good advice when it comes to investing your money, but it's terrible advice for investing your soul. It's okay to put all your eggs in one basket if the basket is labeled *Jesus*.

Some years ago a Christian apologist debated a well-known Muslim in South Africa. At one point the Muslim tried to ridicule the Christian faith by saying that Christians are riding on the back of a crucified man. The Christian answered by saying, "You're right. We're riding on the back of a crucified man, and He is going to take us all the way to heaven."

First John 1:7 says, "The blood of Jesus, [God's] Son, purifies us from every sin." Jesus is the way to heaven. His blood is the price of admission. When He died on the cross, He cried out, "It is finished" (John 19:30), which means "Paid in full."

Take Me to the Cross

In one of his sermons during the Global Mission in Puerto Rico, Billy Graham told the following story. There was a patrolman on night duty in a town in northern Britain. As he walked the streets, he heard a quivering sob. Shining his flashlight into the darkness, he saw a little boy in the shadows sitting on a doorstep, tears running down the lad's cheek. The child said, "I'm lost. Please take me home." And the policeman began naming street after street, trying to help the boy remember where he lived. He named the shops and the hotels in the area, but the little boy could give him no clue.

Then the bobby remembered that at the center of the town there was a church with a large white cross, and that cross towered high above the rest of the city. The policeman pointed to the cross and said, "Do you live anywhere near that place?" The little boy's face immediately brightened. "Yes, sir. Take me to the cross, and I can find my way home."

The cross is God's provision for man's sin. If you are lost and confused, the cross of Christ beckons you to come, repent of your sin, and receive Christ. If you go to the cross, you will find your way home to God.[4]

THE RESULT OF FORGIVENESS

Recently I discovered there are four important words for forgiveness in the Bible—three Hebrew words and one Greek word. The first Hebrew word means "to cover"—like using a rug to cover the dirt on your floor. The second word means to lift and take away—which happens when you remove a stain from a carpet. The third word means to pardon or to wipe the record clean. The fourth word means to "let go" or to "send away"—as when you release a prisoner from jail.[5]

When you put these words together, you get a graphic picture of forgiveness. *God covers our sin, He removes the inner stain, He wipes our personal record clean, and then He releases us from the guilt so that we are set free.*

The Bible uses a number of word pictures to help us grasp the concept of forgiveness. "Blessed is he whose transgressions are forgiven, whose sins are covered" (Psalm 32:1). "As far as the east is from the west, so far has he removed our transgressions from us" (Psalm 103:12). One of the most beautiful gospel promises is found in Isaiah 43:25: "I, even I, am he who blots out your transgressions, for my own sake, and remembers yours sins no more."

A Cop's Cop

I've never forgotten a police officer I met in the first church I pastored, in Southern California. He had been a cop's cop. He was tough with a capital *T*. He had seen the underside of life, and it had left him jaded and skeptical. Before he was a cop he had served in Vietnam and had seen some horrible things. I think that's what made him live "on the edge."

He lived right across the street from our church, his children occasionally came to Sunday school, and he and his wife would sometimes show up for a worship service. Over the months we struck up a friendship—mostly because he told the most incredible stories I'd ever heard in my life. He was what you would call a "seeker." For a long time, he just plied me with one question after another about the Bible and Jesus Christ. He wasn't hostile or negative but was sincerely looking for the truth.

One day we went to eat at a little hole-in-the-wall restaurant where they made the best tacos in town. He said, "Let me tell you what happened to me." And he proceeded to tell me that after thinking about it for a long time, he had recently given his heart to Jesus Christ. "As I was reading the Bible, suddenly it hit me, 'This stuff is true!'" Then he told me how he had asked Christ to become his Savior and Lord. I will never forget his description of that moment: "It felt like a thousand pounds were lifted off my shoulders."

That's what it means to have peace with God. The weight of sin is lifted off your shoulders. The guilt is gone because your sins have been forgiven.

THE COST OF FORGIVENESS

To speak of the cost of forgiveness may sound strange to those who understand the doctrine of the grace of God. Does the Bible not speak of salvation as a free gift? Indeed it does: "For it is by grace you have been saved, through faith—and this not from yourselves, it is the gift of God—not by works, so that no one can boast" (Ephesians 2:8-9). In fact, that text clearly states that salvation comes to us as a gift precisely so that we might not boast that we did anything to earn it.

As we have already seen, it is the blood of Christ that provides the ground of our forgiveness. If Jesus really did pay it all, how then can there be any cost to us? Is forgiveness free or it is not free? The answer is, it depends on how you look at it.

From God's side, salvation is provided for you and me free of charge because Jesus paid the price at the cross. We couldn't pay enough to atone for even one of our sins. Someone had to pay the debt we owed. That someone was Jesus.

Between the Sinner and God

But from our side, the picture is quite different. What will it cost you to have your sins forgiven? Presbyterian theologian John Gerstner said that the only thing standing between the sinner and God is the sinner's virtue.[6] The sinner always thinks he is better than he really is and that he's not as bad as he really is. He has it wrong both ways. In God's eyes the sinner is not so hot after all; even his presumed righteousness is like "filthy rags" in God's eyes (Isaiah 64:6).

But that's why many people will never be saved. They think they're better than they really are. And because they won't give up that false notion of their own goodness, they can never be forgiven.

You Need 1,000 Points

The story is told of a very good man who one day died and appeared at the pearly gates. He had lived such a good life that he presumed the gates would automatically swing open for him and he would soon be relaxing in his heavenly mansion. When he rang the buzzer, St. Peter came to meet him. When the man said he wanted to live in heaven, St. Peter said, "Very well, but you need 1,000 points to enter heaven." The man smiled, knowing that his good works would certainly surpass that total. "During my life I volunteered for the Red Cross and the Community Chest and gave money to every charitable organization in town." "Excellent," said St. Peter. "You get one point."

Somewhat taken aback, the man continued, "I was a faithful family man. I was married to the same woman for forty years. I loved my four children and sent them to the finest schools." "Oh my," St. Peter replied, "we don't get many like you up here. That's another point." Now sweating profusely, the man said, "I was a Scout leader, I attended church every Sunday, I served on the board, I sang in the choir, I taught Sunday school." "Commendable in every way. What a credit you were to the community. That's another point. Let's see now. Your total is three points."

Falling on his knees, the man cried out in desperation, "But for the grace of God, no one can get into heaven." To which St. Peter replied, "You have just received 1,000 points."[7]

To be saved, you must first realize that you can't save yourself. As long as you hold onto your self-righteousness, you cannot be forgiven. One of our old hymns puts it this way: "Nothing in my hand I bring, simply to Thy cross I cling."[8] That image of the empty hand is appropriate because it pictures exactly how we must come to God. We come with empty hands or we don't come at all.

"WHY SHOULD I LET YOU INTO MY HEAVEN?"

With that we return to our original question. Did Mickey Mantle go to heaven? In spite of his fame and fortune, at the end his hands were empty. All those home runs and all those amazing catches and even that wonderful Oklahoma smile couldn't forgive even one of his sins. By his own admission, he came to the end of his life with many sins that needed forgiveness.

Bobby Richardson and his wife went back to visit Mickey Mantle the day before he died. Mrs. Richardson asked Mickey a very pointed question: "If you were to stand before God and he said to you, 'Why should I let you into my heaven?' what would you say?" He immediately replied with the words of John 3:16, "For God so loved the world, that he gave his only begotten Son, that whosoever believeth in him should not perish, but have everlasting life."

That's the right answer. Did Mickey Mantle go to heaven? I believe the answer is yes. He reached out with the empty hands of faith and took hold of Jesus Christ. The blood of Jesus Christ cleansed him from all his sins.

Let's think again about the man who needed 1,000 points to get to heaven. It's a good story, but it's partly untrue. Once you die, it's too late to receive forgiveness. No one will get a second chance at the gates of heaven. Mickey Mantle almost waited too long.

So let me ask a very personal question. Have you ever come to Jesus Christ and had your sins forgiven? Has there ever been a definite moment when you repented of your sins and asked Jesus Christ to be your Savior?

STANDING AT THE CROSSROAD

As you read this chapter you are standing at a crossroad. This is your moment to make a choice for Jesus or against Him. If this were a Billy Graham crusade, I would ask you to come forward and stand at the front while all of us were singing.

I want to share with you a simple prayer of commitment to Christ. You need to know that prayer alone can't save you. Only Jesus can save you. But you will be saved if you reach out to Him by faith. If this is the prayer of your heart, say it to God right now.

> Lord Jesus, I know I'm a sinner. Thank You for dying on the cross for me. I truly believe You are the Son of God who rose from the dead. Here and now I repent of my sin, and I trust You as my Lord and Savior. Come into my heart, Lord Jesus. I ask You to make me a new person. In Jesus' name, Amen.

Being a Christian means coming to Christ for salvation. It means leaving your sin behind and leaning completely on Christ by faith, trusting totally in Him. He then comes into your heart, forgives your sin, and changes your way of life. The cross of Christ is your only hope of heaven. You must come by faith because that's the only way a guilty sinner can come to God.

There is bad news and good news in the Gospel. The bad news is that you are a sinner desperately in need of forgiveness. The good news is that through Christ all your sins can be forgiven forever.

Christians believe in the forgiveness of sins through the blood of Jesus Christ. Apart from Jesus, God has no other plan and you have no other hope.

SOMETHING TO THINK ABOUT

Don't try to deal with sin, for you are sure to lose. Deal with Christ; let him deal with your sin and you are sure to win.

—ARTHUR H. ELFSTRAND

QUESTIONS TO CONSIDER

1. Do you agree that the entire human race is sinful? What evidence of sin do you see in your own life?

2. Do you ever worry, like Mickey Mantle did, that when you die, God won't let you into heaven? What reason would God have *not* to let you in?

3. What is the difference between believing *about* Jesus and believing *in* Him?

4. Do you truly believe that salvation comes only through faith in Christ? What about those who choose to follow other religions? What about those who never hear about Jesus at all?

5. When Jesus cried out, "It is finished," what did He mean?

6. According to John Gerstner, what is the only thing standing between a sinner and God? What—if anything—stands between you and God right now?

SCRIPTURES TO PONDER

Isaiah 53

Acts 10:43

Romans 5:12-21

Seven

POSTCARDS FROM THE EDGE

What a Christian Believes About Angels and Demons

Angels are in. In the words of the *Wall Street Journal*, "After a hiatus of almost 300 years and much skepticism, angels are making a comeback."[1] A recent survey confirmed this fact: 58 percent of Americans in households making over $50,000 believe in angels, as do 55 percent of college graduates, 54 percent of working mothers, and 51 percent of parents with children under the age of eight. These are the affluent consumers who have snapped up angel earrings and helped propel books on angels into best-sellers.[2]

Ten years ago you could hardly find a single book on angels in a secular bookstore. Now you can find dozens. Angels are definitely in. But so are demons. *Newsweek* magazine reports that two out of three Americans believe the devil exists.[3] A recent Gallup poll in Canada, for example, revealed that from 1985 to 1995 belief in God slipped from 87 percent to 70 percent; but during the same time period belief in the devil rose from 33 percent to 54 percent.[4]

If you doubt the popularity of Satan and his demons, go into any Christian bookstore and you will find at least twenty books in print on this subject. In fact, it seems to me that, for the Christian public at least, demons interest us far more than angels.

That shouldn't surprise us, however. Bad news always travels faster than good news. That's why our ten o'clock newscasts almost always begin with a robbery or a murder or a conviction or a terrible accident.

Angels may be more important, but they aren't nearly as interesting as demons.

OUR ONLY RELIABLE SOURCE

In this chapter I'd like to survey the biblical evidence for angels and demons. Right up front, I need to make one point very clear. *Our only reliable source of information regarding the spirit world is the Bible.* Many people claim to have had personal experience with angels and demons—or with what they believed to be angels or demons—but those experiences must be judged by the written Word of God, the Bible. Everything that we know for certain is found in God's Word.[5]

That fact shouldn't discourage you since the Bible has a great deal to say about angels and demons. In fact, they are mentioned in thirty-four different books of the Bible in over 300 different places. You will find the first angels in Genesis 3, the first demons in Deuteronomy 32, the last demons in Revelation 16, and the last angels in Revelation 22.[6] Therefore, we have plenty of material to study, far more in fact than we could cover in one chapter of this book.

ANGELS AMONG US

Who are the angels? Here is a five-part answer: They are:

- Created beings.

- Spirit beings.
- Personal beings.
- Immortal beings.
- Powerful beings.

The angels are real beings created by God who, because they are spirit beings, are normally invisible to the human eye. According to the Bible, the total number of angels is beyond all human computation. Often they are referred to by such terms as "the host of heaven," "the joyful assembly" and "the mighty ones." When God created the universe, He created a vast number of angelic creatures at the same time.

Two unfallen angels are named in the Bible—Michael the archangel and Gabriel, who is something like a divine press secretary. For instance, he's the one who announced to Mary that she would give birth to Jesus the Messiah (Luke 1:26-38). Furthermore, it appears that the angels are organized into various groups. For instance, the Bible speaks of the cherubim and the seraphim. It also uses terms such as "thrones," "powers," and "authorities" to describe the various ranks of angels.

However, the Bible doesn't reveal everything we'd like to know. As we study the angels, we are like an audience waiting for a play to begin. As the houselights go down, you can see feet moving beneath the curtains, and from time to time the curtains rustle as someone brushes them from the rear. Occasionally you see eyes peering out from the wings. So you know someone is back there. But how many people and what they look like or what they are doing, you cannot say for certain. That must wait until the curtain finally rises and the play begins. Our knowledge of angels is small compared to the vast reality that is hidden from our eyes.[7]

WHAT ANGELS DO

What exactly do angels do? The Bible pictures angels as fulfilling four great roles.

1. *They worship God in heaven.* This is the most familiar picture of angels in the Bible. Most often when we see them, they are worshiping God. For instance, when Christ was born, the shepherds heard the heavenly host singing, "Glory to God in the highest, and on earth peace to men on whom his favor rests" (Luke 2:14). Though all the angels praise God, some angels are apparently assigned to this as a permanent duty.

2. *They serve as messengers for God.* This is what the Greek word translated *angel* means. An angel is a messenger for the Almighty. Genesis 28 tells of Jacob's amazing dream of a staircase reaching from earth to heaven, with the angels of God descending and ascending on it. That dream demonstrates the close connection that exists between heaven and earth. Though we don't ordinarily see that staircase, it's always there, and the angels constantly go back and forth. I believe the angels ascend to heaven with our prayers in their hands and come back to earth with God's answers for His children.

3. *They war against Satan and his demons.* We see this most clearly in the book of Revelation, but you have glimpses of it in other places in the Bible, most notably Daniel 10. In that passage, a heavenly being was hindered from coming to Daniel because he was

contending with "the prince of the Persian kingdom," evidently a demon who had strong influence over the government of Persia. But then Michael the archangel intervened, and the demon was defeated. Similarly, Revelation 12:7 paints a dramatic picture of an event yet future to us: "And there was war in heaven. Michael and his angels fought against the dragon, and the dragon and his angels fought back." The next verse tells us that Satan will be defeated and his army expelled from heaven once and for all. Please note a crucial fact. *Whenever angels and demons go to war, the angels of God always win because God is greater than Satan.*

4. *They offer special protection to God's people.* Psalm 34:7 says, "The angel of the LORD encamps around those who fear him, and he delivers them." There are many cases of miraculous angelic deliverance in the Bible. When Lot was attacked in Sodom, the two angels struck the unruly mob with blindness. When Daniel was thrown into the lion's den, an angel closed the mouths of the lions so they wouldn't harm him. When Peter was thrown in jail in Acts 12, an angel came to set him free.

TWO CRUCIAL QUESTIONS

Several questions might be asked at this point.

What about guardian angels? Some people believe that each individual is assigned a guardian angel at birth. When Peter came to the door in Acts 12, the disciples didn't believe it was him. They thought it was "his angel" (verse 15). The Bible doesn't specifically teach that we each have one particular guardian angel. However, Jesus in Matthew 18:10, speaking of little children, does say, "Their angels in heaven always see the face of my Father in heaven." We do know from Hebrews 1:14 that angels are "ministering spirits sent to serve" Christians. But the Bible does not specifically say whether or not we each have an assigned angel. I am inclined to agree with John Calvin who suggested that we have guardian angels, but more than one each. The Bible speaks of "the host of heaven"—whole armies of angels watching over God's people. I like that idea. Perhaps God has a platoon of Angelic Special Forces watching over you right this moment.[8]

Can I encounter an angel today? I think the answer is yes, though you probably wouldn't know it when it happened. Most of the time angels work behind the scenes. When my son and his friends wrecked our van, the owner of the body shop told us it was a miracle someone wasn't killed. The van hit the tree directly in the middle of the front bumper. If the collision point had been one foot to the left or right, at least one person and perhaps more would have been killed. When a close friend heard the story, he said, "An angel took the hit." Based on what the Bible says, that may very well be true.

There is another way in which we might encounter an angel today. Hebrews 13:2 reminds us to entertain strangers gladly, "for by so doing some people have entertained angels without knowing it." This verse refers to Genesis 18 where we read that Abraham served lunch to three strangers, only later to realize that they had been angelic visitors.

We won't know until we get to heaven how much the angels of God have done to protect us, and we'll never know how many times we met angels and didn't know it.

DEMONS ON THE LOOSE

Who or what are demons? The answer is very simple. *Demons are fallen angels—angels that rebelled against God.* The five attributes of angels are therefore also true of demons. When God created the universe, He created a vast array of angelic beings. The most glorious angel was a being named Lucifer, which means "Morning Star." Isaiah 14:12-14 describes in poetic terms how he led a rebellion in heaven in an attempt to overthrow God. That rebellion failed, but in the process a third of the angels followed Lucifer in his evil scheme. Lucifer became the devil, and the rebellious angels became the demons.

The Bible tells us that Satan set up his headquarters right here on Planet Earth. He won his first victory when he convinced Eve to eat the fruit, and she in turn gave it to Adam and he ate. Thus sin entered paradise. From that moment until this, the whole world has been the devil's playground, and the demons have been his foot soldiers in his great battle against God.

EVIL THROUGH AND THROUGH

Demons have only one purpose: to further Satan's evil work in the world. They are evil through and through; they hate God, and they hate Jesus Christ. They are unholy, disobedient, arrogant liars. Like Satan, they come only to steal, kill, and destroy. And like him, they work through the world and the flesh to tempt us to do wrong.

The Old Testament doesn't say much about demons. However, we know from Deuteronomy 32:17 that demons were connected

with pagan idolatry. That's why the people of Israel were repeatedly warned against any form of sorcery, witchcraft, or anything
occult. All of it was strictly forbidden.[9]

Most of what the Bible says about demons comes from the
Gospel accounts of the life of Jesus. Time and again Jesus encoun-
tered men and women who had somehow fallen under the control
of demonic spirits. Some of the terrible afflictions wrought by
demons included blindness, deafness, loss of speech, paralysis,
insanity, seizures, and suicidal tendencies. Interestingly, the Bible
never connects demon possession with personal moral sin.[10] In fact,
the Gospel writers seem to put it in the category of sickness and dis-
ease. It's also worth noting that whenever Jesus cast out a demon,
it came out instantly because the demons must bow before the
mighty name of the Son of God.

FOUR CRUCIAL QUESTIONS

Let me answer a few questions that may help focus our thinking.

Are demons at work in the world today? Absolutely. In fact, the
Bible seems to indicate that demonic activity will increase as we
near the end of the age.[11] I think demons especially work through
Satanism, occultic games, seances, the New Age movement,
Eastern religions, sexual perversion of every kind (including homo-
sexuality), drug abuse, pornography, and idolatry.

*Is it possible for a person to be demon-possessed in the same sense in
which the Bible uses the term?* In my judgment, the answer is yes and
no. Yes, unbelievers can be "possessed" or fully controlled by
demons. After all, if you don't know Christ as Savior, you are

already living in Satan's kingdom. As an unholy sovereign, he can do as he wishes with his subjects.[12]

But I believe the answer is quite different for the Christian. I do not believe that a Christian can be "possessed" or "demonized" in the same sense in which the New Testament uses those terms. I believe such a notion flies in the face of the biblical teaching regarding our position in Christ, the complete forgiveness of our sins, the power of the blood of Christ, the indwelling Holy Spirit, and the absolute promise of God's Word that "greater is he that is in you, than he that is in the world" (1 John 4:4, *King James Version*). If God is in us, there is no room for the demons, because God will not share his children with the Evil One. And he won't give the devil "squatter's rights" either.

How do demons attack believers today? The answer is, they attack us through our minds by suggesting thoughts that may lead us into sin and spiritual compromise. Second Corinthians 10:5 challenges us to "take captive every thought to make it obedient to Christ." We do that by yielding our mind to Christ and by consciously and continually obeying Philippians 4:8, which says: "Whatever is true, whatever is noble, whatever is right, whatever is pure, whatever is lovely, whatever is admirable—if anything is excellent or praiseworthy—think about such things." Every moment of every day your mind is a battleground between good and evil.

As believers we must constantly be on guard lest through a careless and undisciplined thought life we unwittingly fall prey to Satan's subtle attacks.

GET RID OF THE MANURE!

Suppose you woke up one morning and discovered a half-ton of fresh manure on your front lawn. The manure not only smells terrible, it also attracts a thick cloud of ugly flies that buzz around you whenever you go outdoors.

How could you ever get rid of the flies? There are two possible answers to that question. First, you could try to catch the flies one by one, naming them, classifying them, ranking them, figuring out who the head fly is and who his top lieutenants are. You could even write papers on "How to Get Rid of Flies" or "Understanding the Hierarchy of Flies" or "Discerning the Flies in Your Family Tree." That's one way to handle the problem.

Or you could just get out there with a shovel, load the manure into a truck, and haul it away. When the manure is gone, the flies will leave too.

That illustration graphically shows how Christians should deal with demons. Get rid of the manure in your life, and the demons will leave you alone.

James 4:7 says, "Resist the devil, and he will flee from you." He also tells us exactly how to do that:

- "Submit" to God in every area of your life, verse 7.
- "Come near to God" in prayer and worship, verse 8.
- Confess your sins, verse 8.
- "Purify" your heart, verse 8.
- Weep over your sin, verse 9.
- "Humble yourselves before the Lord," verse 10.

Then we have the promise: "And he will lift you up." It is never

God's will for any believer to live in bondage to demons—not even for a moment. *If you want to, you can be free from Satan's power in your life.* But you must stand and fight the good fight of faith. You must take up the armor of God every day. And above all else, you must start taking personal responsibility for your own life. As long as you keep making excuses for the manure in your life, you leave yourself open to demonic attack.

STRIKING A BIBLICAL BALANCE

As we think about the spirit realm and how we should relate to it, here are four principles that will help us stay balanced and biblical.

Base Your Faith on the Bible, Not Human Experience

At this point I would repeat again that the only reliable source of information is the Word of God. *The Bible tells us absolutely everything we need to know in this area.* Unfortunately, many people turn to human experience to fill in the blanks. This is a grave mistake because you end up with an elaborate theory of angels and demons that doesn't come from the Bible.

Again, we want to believe everything the Bible says about the spirit world—nothing more, nothing less, nothing else.

Remember That Both Angels and Demons Are Completely Under God's Control

Martin Luther believed fervently in the devil, even to the point that he sometimes would throw his inkwell at the wall in order to get rid of him. But it was Luther who rightly said that the devil is "God's devil," meaning that he is completely under God's control. For reasons we do not understand, God has allowed Satan to wreak havoc in the universe. But remember the story of Job in the Old Testament. Satan had to ask God's permission before he attacked Job. Remember too Luke 22:31, where we read that Jesus said to Peter, "Satan has asked to sift you as wheat." Satan can do nothing without God's allowing it. He cannot touch a child of God unless God gives the okay.[13]

That is why 1 John 5:18 says that "the evil one" (Satan) cannot harm a child of God. The Greek word used in that verse means to do permanent, lasting, irreparable harm. Satan and his demons can harass us, oppress us, confuse us, disturb us, mislead us, trick us, and discourage us. But in the end we will stand like champions before the throne of God and say, "He never laid a glove on me." He can slow us down, but he can't stop us. He can discourage us, but he can't defeat us. He can knock us down, but he can't keep us down, because by God's grace we will get up to fight again. He can take away our assurance, but he can't take away our salvation, because the Holy Spirit has taken up permanent residence within the heart of every believer.

Let This Truth Increase Your Confidence in God

Be encouraged, child of God! *We're on the winning side*. In the end Satan will be judged and cast into the lake of fire. The Bible says that he walks about "like a roaring lion" (1 Peter 5:8). But lions often roar because they are old and toothless. Satan's greatest weapon is fear. He enslaves millions of people through the fear of death.

Years ago Stanley Collins, then director of the Forest Home Conference Center, came to speak at the church I served as pastor in Downey, California. While preaching on Paul's magnificent words, "Where, O death, is your victory? Where, O death, is your sting?" (1 Corinthians 15:55), he told us about an occasion during World War II when, as a young officer in the British Army, he and some friends came upon an unexploded German artillery shell. Immediately they called in the experts, who disarmed it. Later that night he walked into his room and found a friend using the shell as a pillow. Once the fuse had been removed, the shell was harmless.

We still die, but Christ has taken the sting out of death. We still fight Satan, but we fight from a position of victory, because Jesus Christ won the battle 2,000 years ago. We still struggle with temptation, but we don't have to give in, because God has provided the way of escape. We face many hardships in this life, but we know that all things work together for good to those who love God, who are called according to His purpose (Romans 8:28). We may be filled with doubts and think ourselves unworthy of God's love, and we may fear that God will get angry and cast us off; but we are more than conquerors through Him who loved us.

Use the Weapons God Has Given You

What are the weapons of our warfare against Satan? Paul spelled them out for us in Ephesians 6:10-17. You may be familiar with the passage. It begins this way:

Be strong in the Lord and in his mighty power. Put on the full armor
of God so that you can take your stand against the devil's schemes.
For our struggle is not against flesh and blood, but against the rulers,
against the authorities, against the powers of this dark world and
against the spiritual forces of evil in the heavenly realms. Therefore
put on the full armor of God, so that when the day of evil comes, you
may be able to stand your ground, and after you have done every-
thing, to stand.

Do you want to know God's will for your life? God's will is that
you stand in the evil day. He has given you the armor. Put it on and
take your place on the firing line.

And what is the armor of God?

- It's "the belt of truth."
- It's "the breastplate of righteousness."
- It's the shoes of "the gospel of peace."
- It's "the shield of faith."
- It's "the helmet of salvation."
- It's "the sword of the Spirit . . . the word of God."

God armor is comprised of resting in God's truth, living a righ-
teous life, walking in God's peace, living by faith, relying on your
salvation, standing on the mighty power of God's Word. Then Paul
wraps it up with one final ingredient: prayer. Verse 18 says, "Pray
in the Spirit on all occasions with all kinds of prayers and requests.
With this in mind, be alert and always keep on praying for all the
saints."

Here, then, are the Christian's tools for spiritual victory: *truth, righ-*
teousness, peace, faith, salvation, the Word of God, and prayer. Wear this
armor every day and you will not—indeed you cannot—be defeated.

ONE LITTLE WORD

Martin Luther wrote many hymns, one of which was called the "Battle Hymn of the Reformation." After 450 years we still sing it. We know it as "A Mighty Fortress Is Our God." Martin Luther believed in the real existence of Satan and his demons, but he believed even more in the power of God through Jesus Christ. That's why the third verse reads this way:

> *And though this world with devils filled,*
> *Should threaten to undo us.*
> *We will not fear, for God has willed*
> *His truth to triumph through us.*
> *The Prince of Darkness grim,*
> *We tremble not for him,*
> *His rage we can endure,*
> *For lo, his doom is sure.*
> *One little word shall fell him.*

If you know Jesus Christ, you have every reason to be encouraged. Rejoice and give thanks. We have the Word of God on our side and the Holy Spirit living within us. We're on the winning side!

SOMETHING TO THINK ABOUT

The Scripture says that there is a time to be born and a time to die. And when my time comes an angel will be there to comfort me. He will give me peace and joy even at that most critical hour, and usher me into the presence of God, and I will dwell in the house of the Lord forever.

—BILLY GRAHAM

QUESTIONS TO CONSIDER

1. How do you account for the high level of interest in angels in recent years? Do you believe this signals a new interest in spirituality in general?

2. Do you agree that the Bible is our only reliable source of information about the spirit world? What are the dangers of relying on personal experience in this area?

3. What role do angels play in the lives of Christians today? Do you believe in guardian angels? Why or why not? Have you had an experience that might have been an angelic encounter?

4. What role do demons play in the world today? How can demons attack Christians?

5. Is there any "manure" in your life that you need to get rid of?

6. Which part of the "armor of God" do you most need at this very moment?

SCRIPTURES TO PONDER

Genesis 18:1-15 and Hebrews 13:2
2 Corinthians 4:4
Ephesians 6:10-18

Eight

PAYDAY SOMEDAY

What a Christian Believes About Heaven and Hell

In this chapter we come face to face with the most basic question of all: What happens when we die? For thousands of years men and women have pondered this question and have offered differing answers. The *materialist* says there is no such thing as a soul or spirit; so when we die, we simply cease to exist. The *reincarnationist* believes that after we die, we come back to earth in another life form, either higher or lower depending on how we have lived in this life. The *universalist* argues that since a loving God would never send anyone to hell, everyone eventually ends up in heaven. The *second-chance salvationist* says that those who didn't believe in Christ in this life get a second chance after death. The *annihilationist* says that believers go to heaven, while unbelievers are destroyed by God. The *probationist* believes that everyone goes to a place called purgatory where we pay for our own sinful acts until we have purged ourselves, and then we enter heaven.[1]

The question of an afterlife is an ancient one. Job 14:14 asks, "If a man dies, will he live again?" At every funeral that question is asked in one way or another. Is there life after death? If so, what

happens when we die? How can we be sure? And most impor-
tantly, how can we be ready when the moment comes?

What about heaven? What about hell? Are these real places, or
are they merely symbols that point to the universal longing for
immortality? Can we still believe in heaven and hell?

AMERICANS BELIEVE IN HEAVEN AND HELL

A 1991 survey commissioned by *U.S. News and World Report*
shows that 78 percent of Americans believe in heaven, and 60
percent believe in hell. The survey also revealed that 81 percent
of the women surveyed thought they had an excellent chance of
going to heaven, while only 3 percent thought they had a similar
chance of going to hell. "And in heaven as on earth, women will
outnumber men: 73 percent of the guys surveyed say they expect
to go to heaven, while 5 percent say they expect to wind up in
hell."[2]

So most Americans believe in heaven, and most of us are planning on going there. Most of us also believe in hell, but almost no
one expects to go there.

ONLY ONE SOURCE

But we can't base our hope for the future on opinion polls. *We need
to know the truth.* Is there a heaven and a hell? If so, we need to know
what they are really like. And we need to know who is going where
and why.

In all the world there is only one source of authoritative information about the afterlife. Outside of the Bible, everything else is only speculation and wishful thinking. We will not spend any time in this chapter talking about near-death experiences, whether by believers or unbelievers.[3] We want to know what God's Word has to say on this important topic.

Consider first the words of Jesus Christ: "A time is coming when all who are in their graves will hear his voice and come out— those who have done good will rise to live, and those who have done evil will rise to be condemned" (John 5:28- 29). Here we have the testimony of our Lord on the subject. One of two destinies awaits each human being after death: eternal life in heaven or eternal condemnation in hell.

HEAVEN: ETERNAL JOY

Let's consider three important questions relating to heaven.

Where Is Heaven?

There are three things I can tell you in answer to this question. *The most important is that heaven is a real place.* Listen to the words of Jesus on the night before He was crucified:

> "Do not let your hearts be troubled. Trust in God; trust also in me. In my Father's house are many rooms; if it were not so, I would have told you. I am going there to prepare a place for you. And if I go and prepare a place for you, I will come back and take you to be with me that you also may be where I am going. You know the way to the place where I am going."
>
> —JOHN 14:1-3, EMPHASIS MINE

Three times in four verses Jesus calls heaven a place. He means that heaven ("my Father's house") is a real place, as real as New York, London, or Chicago. The place called heaven is just as real as the place you call home. It's a real place filled with real people, which is why the Bible sometimes compares heaven to a mansion with many rooms (John 14:1-3) and sometimes to an enormous city teeming with people (Revelation 21—22).

The Bible also tells us that *heaven is the dwelling place of God.* His throne is there, the angels are there, and the Lord Jesus Christ Himself is in heaven. Philippians 3:20 says very plainly that "our citizenship is in heaven. And we eagerly await a Savior from there, the Lord Jesus Christ." That's why Jesus told the thief crucified beside Him, "Today you will be with me in paradise" (Luke 23:43).

Third (and I find this fact fascinating), the Bible hints that *heaven is not as far away as we might think.* Because heaven is a real place, we sometimes think it must be outside our present universe—which would mean it is billions and billions of light-years away. However, it's very clear that the early Christians understood that they would pass *immediately* from this life into the presence of Christ in heaven. How can that be possible if heaven is beyond the farthest galaxy? Hebrews 12:22-24 tells us something amazing about what the Gospel has done for us:

> *But you have come to Mount Zion, to the heavenly Jerusalem, the city of the living God. You have come to thousands upon thousands of angels in joyful assembly, to the church of the firstborn, whose names are written in heaven. You have come to God, the judge of all men, to the spirits of righteous men made perfect, to Jesus the medi-*

*ator of a new covenant, and to the sprinkled blood that speaks a bet-
ter word than the blood of Abel.*

The writer is comparing Mt. Sinai with Mt. Zion. Under the Old
Covenant no one could come near God except under very strict
conditions. That's why the mountain shook with thunder and lightning. But now in Christ we have been brought near to heavenly
realities.[4] Think of what He is saying:

- We're not that far from heaven.
- We're not that far from the angels.
- We're not that far from our loved ones in heaven.
- We're not that far from God.
- We're not that far from Jesus Himself.

Heaven is a real place. It's where Jesus is right now, and it's not
far away from us.

Who Is in Heaven Right Now?

This question is not difficult to answer. God is in heaven because
heaven is His dwelling-place. The Lord Jesus has been in heaven
ever since He ascended from the earth, shortly after His resurrection (Acts 1:9-11). The Bible tells us that angels are in heaven. In fact,
there are myriads of angels—uncountable numbers of heavenly
beings—all of them serving the Lord in various ways.

And the saints of God who died on this earth are in heaven.[5] The
Bible teaches that the moment we die, we go directly into the presence of the Lord Jesus Christ. Paul spoke of this in 2 Corinthians 5:7-
8 and Philippians 1:21-23.

But I do not want to be ambiguous on this point. *Not everyone who has died is in heaven.* Some people won't make it. The Bible speaks of the saved and the lost. The saved are those who trust Jesus Christ as their eternal Savior. The lost are those who do not trust Christ as Savior. This is the great dividing line of humanity—you are either saved or you are lost. And there is no middle category. You will either spend eternity in heaven or eternity in hell.

I simply want you to know what God has said about heaven and who will go there. The saved of all the ages will be there, and that vast throng will no doubt include many people who would surprise us if we knew it now. Certainly heaven will be more wonderful than we can imagine and its population more diverse than we expect.

But I am sure of this one truth: *No one will go to heaven except by the grace of God and through the merits of the blood of Jesus Christ.* If a man says no to Jesus, he has no hope of heaven.

Will We Know Each Other in Heaven?

This is one of the most frequently asked questions about heaven. I would like to share an answer given by a Bible teacher of another generation—a man named William Pettingill:[6] "We may be sure that we shall not know less in heaven than we know here." As proof he quotes 1 Corinthians 13:12, "For now we see through a glass darkly, but then face to face: now I know in part; but then shall I know even as also I am known" (*King James Version*). How does God know us? He knows us completely, intimately, thoroughly, inside and out, with nothing hidden but rather everything seen as it really is (Psalm 139:1-4, Hebrews 4:12-13). When we get to heaven we'll know each other as God knows us, because all the imperfections of this life will be removed. In this life sin causes us to cover ourselves—not just physically, but emotionally and spiritually. But when sin is finally lifted from us, then we can be ourselves with no shame, no pain, no embarrassment, and no covering up.

In his very helpful book on heaven, W. A. Criswell makes the additional point that individual personality survives into eternity. I'll be the same person then that I am now—but with all the imperfections and limitations of sin finally removed. This is a wonderful thought—that the essence of who we are will remain throughout eternity, yet vastly improved by God's grace.[7]

In heaven we will know each other intimately. That's why on the Mount of Transfiguration Peter, James, and John recognized Moses and Elijah, even though those two Old Testament saints had been dead for hundreds of years (Matthew 17:1-8). I don't think they had name tags on. I think there was something about those two men that made Peter, James, and John recognize them even though they'd never seen them before.

That's why a wife whose husband died when she was young will be able to pick her husband out of a crowd of billions of people, even though she hasn't seen him for fifty years. In heaven she'll say, "Sweetheart! I knew it was you!" And he will know her.

How this can be, I do not know, but I believe it to be true. In heaven there will be no strangers.

HELL: ETERNAL MISERY

We turn now to consider what the Bible says about hell. It may interest you to know that Jesus believed in a literal hell. In fact, He spoke about hell more often than He spoke about heaven. Jesus told a story in Luke 16 about a rich man and a beggar named Lazarus. When Lazarus died he went to heaven, but the rich man went to hell. We pick up the story in verse 23: "In hell, where he was in torment, he looked up and saw Abraham far away, with Lazarus by his side. So he called to him, 'Father Abraham, have pity on me and send Lazarus to dip the tip of his finger in water and cool my tongue, because I am in agony in this fire.'" Some people have great difficulty with this story because they reject the notion that Jesus believed in a literal hell with literal fire. But here Jesus plainly says that the rich man was tormented in the fires of hell. I find nothing in the text to suggest that this is symbolic. It appears to be an actual description of hell.

Someone has called hell the "forgotten doctrine" of the evangelical church. We don't talk about it nowadays because it isn't popular to suggest that unbelievers are tormented for all eternity for their sins. In order to soften the blow, some theologians have suggested that unbelievers are annihilated or destroyed by God, and thus they will not suffer throughout eternity. What is the truth?

The Lake of Fire

I confess that the thought of everlasting torment is indeed so gruesome as to be almost unbearable. But the Bible teaches the eternal punishment of the wicked in many passages. The words and phrases the Bible associates with hell include: smoke, fire, burning, torment, bottomless pit, everlasting prison, wrath, weeping, wailing, gnashing of teeth, unquenchable fire, damnation, furnace of fire, blackness and darkness, brimstone.

Revelation 20:11-15 describes the awesome scene surrounding the Great White Throne judgment at the end of time (specifically, the end of Jesus Christ's literal thousand-year reign on the earth). In this passage we discover the final destination of those who will not bow before Jesus Christ as Savior and Lord: "If anyone's name was not found written in the book of life, he was thrown into the lake of fire" (verse 15).

Pause for a moment to let that image settle in your mind. A "lake of fire." *This is the most terrible verse in all the Bible.* What would a lake of fire be like? It is a lake so large that you cannot see the other side. A lake filled with fire and burning smoke. A lake so hot that no one can come near it without burning up. The roar of the fire never stops; the smoke ascends forever. Into that lake the unsaved are tossed one by one, screaming, pleading, begging for mercy. But it is too late. Too late for repentance. Too late for remorse. Too late to give one's heart to Jesus. That day is long past.

The Bible calls this "the second death." It is the final destination of those who left this life without receiving Jesus Christ as their Savior from sin.

If someone objects to my depiction, I assure you that I mean no harm or offense to anyone. But I believe the lake of fire is real. And I am sure that the reality is far worse than my words portray.

WHY IT MUST BE TRUE

Since some people scoff at the notion of an afterlife, let's pause for a moment and ask why the Bible reveals heaven and hell to us. What do we gain by knowing about these things, and why are they important to the Christian faith?

To Right the Wrongs of This Life

What shall we say about the people who get away with murder and then go free? What about the pornographers who ruin so many lives? What about the drug pushers who corrupt our young people? What about the husbands who walk out on their wives for other women? What about the politicians who abuse their power and get rich off the misery of others? What about the monstrous criminal who killed a pregnant mother and her two children and then tore the unborn baby from her body? How can any punishment on earth repay such people for what they have done?

So many crimes go unpunished, while the perpetrators are set free to hurt others. Hell must exist, if for no other reason than to balance the scales of justice.

To Reward Those Who Serve the Lord

As I write these words I'm thinking of a friend of mine, Eva Lodgaard, who has spent more than fifty years as a missionary in the hills of southeastern Kentucky. She started her ministry in 1945 back in the remote regions of the Appalachian Mountains, riding on horseback along the creek beds to teach the Bible to schoolchildren. Eva Lodgaard is not famous as the world counts fame. She could have stayed in suburbia, gotten married, had a family, and enjoyed a comfortable retirement. But she chose to serve the Lord in out-of-the-way places instead.

Where is her reward? I know that she is greatly loved by all who know her—and that is part of her reward—but the best is yet to come. God has promised to reward those who serve Jesus Christ on the earth. Heaven must exist so that those who served Jesus faithfully may enter their eternal reward.

To Fulfill the Promises God Made to His People

The Bible is filled with promises about heaven. Jesus said, "I am going . . . to prepare a place for you. And if I go and prepare a place for you, I will come back and take you to be with me that you may also be where I am" (John 14:3). The last two chapters of the Bible are a description of heaven. Millions of believers have died believing in the reality of heaven. If it's not true, then God is a liar. Heaven must exist because Jesus promised to take us there when we die.

To Redeem the Suffering of This Life

Romans 8:18 says that "our present sufferings are not worth comparing with the glory that will be revealed in us." Not a week goes by that I don't talk with someone whose suffering seems to be overwhelming. Most of the time we can't fully understand why God allows certain things to happen to us. When the books are opened and the scales are balanced, we will discover that the things we went through in this life are nothing compared with the glories of heaven. No one will ever say to Jesus, "Heaven's not so great. It wasn't worth what I went through to get here." When we finally get to heaven, the glory will be so magnificent that we won't even remember the things that made us weep in this life. Heaven must exist, or our present suffering loses its meaning.

WHAT IT ALL MEANS FOR YOU

As I was coming home from my daily walk, I noticed a hearse and funeral procession coming down the street toward one of several cemeteries in our area. It was a clear, crisp, beautiful day, and my first thought was, "I'm glad I don't have to speak at a funeral service today." I kept walking, and within a block another hearse passed me, this time with fewer cars in the procession. A few minutes later a third hearse passed by, with even fewer cars behind it. As I watched the faces of the people in the cars, the thought hit me: "I've done plenty of funerals. Someday I'll be the one in the hearse."

My day is coming, and so is yours. The Bible says, "Man is destined to die once, and after that to face judgment" (Hebrews 9:27). That's one appointment no one will miss. Sooner or later we will all die.

One day you will be the one in the hearse. What will happen then?

When I asked an atheist friend what happens when we die, he said nothing happens. Our bodies are buried, and our soul dissolves into nothingness.

But what if he's wrong?

THE WAGER

Several hundred years ago the French philosopher Pascal put forth his famous wager regarding the Christian faith. It's an imaginary conversation between a Christian and a nonbeliever. It goes like this: Suppose that atheism is right and Christianity is wrong. In the end I have lost nothing by believing in Christ since my faith gives me hope and comfort in this life; and the atheist has gained nothing because he believes that death ends all. But suppose that Christianity is right and atheism is wrong. Who wins and who loses? The Christian wins everything because he goes to heaven. The atheist loses everything because he goes to hell.

If we are wrong, we lose nothing at all. If we are right, we go to heaven. But those who reject Christ run a terrible risk that hell is real because if it is, that's where they are going.[8]

Each person who reads these words must make an intelligent and informed decision about heaven and hell. If what I have said is true, you must do whatever it takes to make sure you go to heaven, and you must make sure at all costs that you do not go to hell.

TWO THINGS I KNOW

Let's go back one more time to the words of Jesus Christ in John 14. When Thomas asked Him the way to heaven, Jesus gave this answer: "I am the way and the truth and the life. No one comes to the Father except through me" (verse 6).

The way to heaven is as narrow as the cross. Only those who trust Jesus Christ as Savior and Lord will enter the gates of heaven.

There are two truths I know about myself with complete certainty: *First, I ought to go to hell because that is where I belong.* In a thousand ways over ten thousand days, I have sinned against God in word and deed. I deserve His punishment because my sins are great. But the second truth is greater than the first: *I am going to heaven because on the cross Jesus Christ paid the price for me; He took my punishment so I could go free.*[9]

GOING TO HELL FROM OAK PARK

Not long ago some friends dropped by the house and gave me a report on some research they'd done into the spiritual history of the town where I live. The cover of their report contained a riveting phrase: "Making it hard to go to hell from Oak Park."[10]

I understand what they meant, but in a sense God has already done that. *He's made it hard to go to hell from Oak Park and from every other community on earth.* Two thousand years ago God put a stop sign on the road to hell. The stop sign is in the shape of a cross. You can ignore it if you wish and take your chances. Or you can stop in your tracks and set out on the road to heaven.

It is said that the road to hell is paved with good intentions. By the same token, the road to heaven is paved with the blood of Christ. Which road are you traveling?

A cartoon from the *Wall Street Journal* shows a successful businessman walking up the stairs toward the gates of heaven. Above the gates is a sign with two words: "No Deals." This time the *Journal* got it absolutely right. God makes no deals when it comes to heaven. You either enter by way of the cross or you don't enter at all.[11]

If you intend to go to heaven, you need to do something about it now. You will live forever somewhere. Will it be in the eternal joy of heaven? Or will you suffer unending misery in hell?

The choice is yours. Choose life. Choose Christ.

SOMETHING TO THINK ABOUT

I'm as sure of heaven as if I'd already been there 10,000 years.

—JACK WYRTZEN

QUESTIONS TO CONSIDER

1. Are you surprised that so many people believe in heaven and hell? What does that say about the spiritual condition of this generation?

2. Why are the reports of near-death experiences not necessarily a reliable guide in thinking about life after death? Have you ever had such an experience or known anyone who did? How did it compare with the teaching of the Bible regarding life after death?

3. "Heaven is a real place." Do you agree? What difference does it make?

4. On what basis will God decide who goes to heaven and who goes to hell?

5. Do you believe hell is a place of eternal torment? What difference does it make?

6. If you died tonight, do you know for certain you would go to heaven? What needs to happen so you can be certain?

SCRIPTURES TO PONDER

Luke 16:19-31
Revelation 20:11-15
Revelation 21:1—22:6

Nine

BEYOND THE CRYSTAL BALL

What a Christian Believes About the Second Coming of Christ

Not long ago *U.S. News and World Report* carried a cover story called "Dark Prophecies." In it the author reported that according to a recent survey 66 percent of Americans believe that Jesus Christ will return to earth someday—including one third of those who say they never attend church. This figure has risen five percentage points in only three years. Why this rise in belief in the Second Coming? The article attributes it—correctly, I believe—to widespread interest in the year 2000.[1]

Forty generations have come and gone since the present millennium began. It is remarkable enough to see a new century— something reserved for our grandparents or (more likely) our great-grandparents; but to witness the passing of one millennium to another—that is something that no one we know has ever seen and no one we know will ever see again.

Because we live at one of the rare moments of history, many people have speculated on what it means for humanity. It's not hard to find apocalyptic imagery on TV and talk radio, in the movies coming out of Hollywood, and in the wave of New Age books that promise a new spirituality for a new millennium. We see it also in worries about the Y2K (Year 2000) computer bug problem that could potentially bring our high-tech society grinding to a halt. And what about the rising tide of Islamic fundamentalism, the continued instability of the former Soviet Union, or the very real threat of nuclear weapons in the hands of a few dedicated terrorists? We could add to that list genuine concern over the moral decline of western society and the complete inability of our leaders to provide lasting answers to our deepest problems.

Are these things signs that we are living in the final days before the end of the world? Is this the "terminal generation" that will see the return of Christ to the earth? Why do two thirds of all Americans now believe in the Second Coming? Is that in itself a "sign" of the Last Days?

Perhaps it is, but remember that Christians have always believed in the Second Coming of Christ. Jesus Himself declared, "I will come back" (John 14:3). And when Christ ascended into heaven, the angels promised the disciples that "this same Jesus, who has been taken from you into heaven, will come back in the same way you have seen him go into heaven" (Acts 1:11). Belief in the Second Coming has always been considered one of the fundamental truths of our faith. Even though we have often argued about the details surrounding His return, Christians of every denomination have agreed on this fact: *Jesus Christ is coming again.*

Perhaps a word of explanation is in order. A *fundamental* doctrine is one that lies at the very heart of our Christian faith. It is a truth so important that not to believe it places you outside the circle of genuine Christianity. Across the centuries only a few doctrines have truly been considered fundamental. Mostly they deal with three areas—the Bible as the Word of God, Jesus as the Son of God, and salvation as a gift of God.[2] Some things simply must be believed if you are to be counted a genuine Christian (and not merely someone following a religion of your own devising). That may seem like a hard statement, but it is true nonetheless. Not everyone who says "Lord, Lord" will enter the Kingdom of Heaven (Matthew 7:21).

In this chapter I want to ask and answer one question: What will the Second Coming of Christ be like? In putting the matter that way, I wish to make clear that my interest is not in detailing "the signs of the times" or in explaining my own views regarding Bible prophecy.[3] My goal is more modest—and perhaps more crucial. What do we Christians mean when we say Christ is coming back? Let's consider three answers to that question.[4]

HIS COMING WILL BE PERSONAL

Acts 1:11 makes it clear that Jesus *Himself* will one day return to the earth. It will be "this same Jesus" who will come again. Twice in one verse (Acts 1:11) Luke uses the word "same" to tell us something crucial about the Second Coming. The "same Jesus" who left will one day return. And He will return "the same way" that He left.

If plain English has any meaning at all, those words teach us that Jesus is coming back personally, literally, visibly, and bodily. We might also add that His coming will be sudden and unexpected. Luke 24:50-52 informs us that as Jesus reached out His hands to bless His disciples, He began to rise from the face of the earth—evidently without any warning whatsoever. We can assume that His return to the earth will be no less astonishing and no less surprising.

This is truly an astounding thought. The same Jesus who was born in Bethlehem is coming again. The same Jesus who grew up in Nazareth is coming again. The same Jesus who turned water into wine is coming again. The same Jesus who walked on water is coming again. The same Jesus who healed the nobleman's son is coming again. The same Jesus who raised Lazarus is coming again. The same Jesus who entered Jerusalem on Palm Sunday is coming again. The same Jesus who wept over Jerusalem is coming again. The same Jesus who was betrayed by Judas is coming again. The same Jesus who was whipped, beaten, scourged, mocked, and condemned to death is coming again. The same Jesus who died on Mount Calvary is coming again. The same Jesus who rose from the dead on Easter Sunday morning is coming again. The same Jesus who ascended into heaven is coming again.[5]

That's what we mean when we say that Jesus is coming again. *The actual, historical figure who lived 2,000 years ago on the other side of the world is returning to the earth one more time.* Kind of blows your mind, doesn't it?

God and Channel 18

Perhaps you've heard about a strange group in Garland, Texas, that announced that God would return to the earth on March 31, 1998. They announced that God would make Himself known by commandeering Channel 18 and announcing His impending arrival on television. At the appointed hour the streets were blocked off so news trucks with their satellite dishes could be there to cover the great event. When asked why he sent a crew, one news director said he didn't expect anything to happen, but he couldn't afford to miss it just in case God showed up on Channel 18.

USA Today ran a rather derisive editorial after God failed to appear on the tube. Later I heard that the group was planning to move to western New York—presumably to try again in a better location.

I have one comment to make. This group—however misguided—was right about one thing. *God in the person of Jesus Christ is coming back someday.* They were wrong about the time, wrong about the place, and were probably wrong about a lot of other things, but on the central point they were right on the money. This world won't continue forever. History will indeed come to a climax when Jesus Himself returns to the earth.

The future will bring an event more marvelous, more startling, more amazing, and more spiritually profound than anything that has happened in the last 2,000 years. I speak of the literal, visible, bodily return of Christ to the earth. *No event may seem less likely to modern men and women; but no event is more certain in the light of inspired Scripture.*

"I will come back," Jesus said (John 14:3). One day those words will be fulfilled before our very eyes.

HIS COMING WILL BE GLORIOUS

Acts 1 tells us that Jesus was caught up in a cloud and taken to heaven. The cloud that carried Jesus into heaven was no ordinary cloud but was in fact the same cloud that led Israel in the wilderness. It is the cloud that represents the glory of God.[6] Luke

21:27 tells us that Jesus will return "in a cloud with power and great glory." Perhaps the best way to understand that statement is to compare the circumstances surrounding the first and second comings. The first time Jesus came unnoticed into the world; the second time "every eye will see him" (Revelation 1:7). In His first coming Jesus humbled Himself, being born in a stable in Bethlehem. When He returns, He will come back as King of kings and Lord of lords. In His first coming He endured the mockery of men who despised Him for His goodness. Although He was the Son of God, He allowed them to put Him to death so He could thereby provide salvation for the world. When He comes again, all mockery will cease, for He will rule the nations with a rod of iron. He came the first time as the Lamb of God; He will come again as the Lion of the Tribe of Judah. Two thousand years ago the religious leaders shouted in scorn, "He saved others, but he can't save himself!" (Matthew 27:42). The day is coming when the whole world will see Jesus as He really is. When that happens, every knee will bow, and every tongue will confess that Jesus Christ is Lord, to the glory of God the Father (Philippians 2:9-11).

Around the first coming inscribe the word HUMILITY in letters large and bold. Around His second coming inscribe the word GLORY that all the world can see. Nothing could be more natural than a triumphant return of our victorious Lord. Though He was once "despised and rejected by men" (Isaiah 53:3), He will one day return "with power and great glory" (Luke 21:27), heralded by angels and accompanied by the saints of every age.

What Will Happen When Christ Returns?

What will occur when Christ returns in glory? First, He will raise the dead in Christ from their graves (1 Thessalonians 4:16). The bodies of dead believers will return to life instantaneously. They will be raised immortal and incorruptible with glorified bodies, like the one Jesus had when He rose on Easter Sunday morning. How will such a great miracle happen? I cannot answer that question but only refer you to this truth: If God can raise His own Son from the dead, He can also raise those who follow His Son.

Second, living believers will be raptured off the face of the earth (1 Thessalonians 4:17). We will be lifted off the earth and changed forever. Our mortal bodies will put on immortality so that we will never die. Jesus will "transform our lowly bodies so that they will be like his glorious body" (Philippians 3:21). Sometimes people say that nothing is as certain as death and taxes. But I know one thing more sure than that: *Some Christians will never die.* One generation— the final one—will be living when Christ returns, and that generation of Christians will never taste death but will be caught up to meet the Lord in the air (see 1 Thessalonians 4:13-18).

Third, Christ will reward His faithful servants when He comes again. Sometimes we say that when a Christian dies, he has "gone to his reward." In one sense that is true, of course. But in the fullest sense, the full reward awaits the moment when we stand before Christ individually to receive His evaluation of what we have done on the earth (2 Corinthians 5:10).

Fourth, when He comes again, Christ will establish His Kingdom and rule over the nations of the world. In the present age the devil is still "the prince of the power of the air" (Ephesians 2:2, *King James Version*) who has usurped Christ's rightful place as King of this earth. That is why the apostle John tells us that "the whole world is under the control of the evil one" (1 John 5:19). One has only to read the headlines each day to know how true this is. How else does one explain a thirteen-year-old and an eleven-year-old opening fire on their classmates in Arkansas? How else can we understand all the greed that causes men to destroy one another? What else could account for broken homes, abortion, homosexuality, adultery, theft, and the flood of immorality flowing like a polluted river across our land? The Bible offers us only this explanation: The devil has hijacked this planet and will not let it go without a fight.

For thousands of years God has been wresting the earth and its people out of Satan's angry grasp. Two thousand years ago Christ defeated the devil when He rose from the dead and ascended to the right hand of God. But that evil spirit keeps fighting even though his doom is sure. When Christ returns, the devil will be defeated once and for all.

Thus the return of Christ will usher in an age of unparalleled peace and prosperity for the world. *A better day is coming for this sin-cursed planet.* When Jesus returns, everyone will know the Lord, from the least to the greatest, from the youngest to the oldest (Jeremiah 31:34). Nations will no longer go to war against each other, and men will beat their swords into plowshares. As the old spiritual says, "Gonna lay down my sword and shield, down by the riverside. Ain't gonna study war no more" (cf. Isaiah 2:1-4). Of such an age the poets have sung, the philosophers have dreamed, and the politicians have waxed eloquent in their promises. It will finally come true when Christ returns in His glory.

HIS COMING IS IMMINENT

The Bible also tells us that the coming of Christ is imminent, which means that it could happen *at any moment*. No matter what else might be said about the writers of the New Testament, and of the first Christians in general, there is no doubt that they all believed that Christ might return in their own generation. This is the normal attitude of Christians in *every* generation. It should be ours as well.

Again and again the New Testament exhorts us to "keep watch" and be ready for His return (Matthew 24:42). Why watch if His coming must be thousands of years away? When Paul uses the phrase, "we who are still alive" in 1 Thessalonians 4:17, he teaches us that the Christian life is best lived in the present tense, expecting at any moment that Jesus might return to the earth.

"I Knew That You Would Come"

The story is told of a businessman who, having an errand to run at his office, took his young son along with him. He asked the boy to wait on the steps while he went inside to do his work. Soon he became so engrossed with his business that he forgot about his son waiting outside. Leaving the building by a different door, he went home alone. Several hours later the family sat down to dinner, but the son was not present. His mother became anxious and wondered where he might be. Then the father remembered where he'd left his son. Hurrying back to his place of work, he found his son, tired and hungry, waiting as he had been instructed to do. "I knew you would come, Father," he said. "You said you would."[7]

Two thousand years have passed since Jesus went to heaven, and some of God's children feel tired and hungry. We wonder why Jesus hasn't come back yet. Perhaps He has forgotten us, we think. Perhaps He made other plans. If you feel like that little boy, take heart. It's been a long time from our point of view, but He's only been gone for two days in heaven's perspective (see 2 Peter 3:8). He said He would come back—*and He will*. Fear not, child of God. Keep believing. He hasn't forgotten you. Soon Christ will return for His own.

With this hope we lay our loved ones to rest in the sacred soil of death. With this hope we rise each morning, look to the eastern sky, and say, "Maybe today." All Christians believe that Jesus will come back someday. He said He would—and He never forgets His promises.

STAY BUSY UNTIL HE RETURNS

Please note that *imminent* does not mean *immediate*. Paul was not mistaken in the least. He expected to see Christ return in his lifetime, and said so. When the word *imminent* is applied to the Second Coming, it means two things: 1) uncertainty as to time, and 2) the possibility of nearness. "Be on guard! Be alert! You do not know when that time will come" (Mark 13:33). This should warn us against the danger of setting dates and reading too much into the "signs" of the end times. We have probably all heard preachers state with great fervency that they believe we are living in the closing moments of world history, the final days before the return of Christ. I feel the same way, but we can't be certain and should not say more than the Bible itself says.

I have already alluded to the fact that Christians differ on the details surrounding the Second Coming. Some questions won't be resolved until Christ comes back. But I would press upon your heart that the points of agreement are far greater than the points of disagreement. All true believers unite in proclaiming our faith that the Lord Himself will one day return to the earth. Consider again the words of the two men dressed in white, "Why do you stand here looking into the sky?" (Acts 1:11). As if to say, "Don't spend your days looking at the clouds, aimlessly dreaming and drifting along." Before Christ left, He told us exactly what to do: We are to be witnesses for Christ to the ends of the earth. After 2,000 years the job is still not done, which means there's enough work to keep us all busy until Jesus comes back.

How can we be ready for Christ's return? Some Christians have answered that question by selling their goods and moving to the wilderness to wait for the Lord. However, Jesus never calls His followers to do such a thing. Instead, He calls us to be faithful in doing whatever He gives us to do.

Your job may be big or small, but whatever it is, do it to the best of your ability and you'll be ready when Jesus returns.

- Be faithful today and you'll be ready today.
- Be faithful tomorrow and you'll be ready tomorrow.
- Be faithful next week and you'll be ready next week.
- Be faithful next year and you'll be ready next year.

Just keep doing what you know to be right, and whenever Jesus comes, you won't be disappointed.

Here is the biblical balance for all of us as we await the return of the Lord:

- Live as though He might come today.
- Plan as though He won't return for a thousand years.

Let me say plainly that I don't know when Jesus will return. I don't know, and I won't set a date. I hope He comes soon. He might come today. I do know this: *Jesus will return when everything is ready in God's plan.* Not a moment earlier, not a second later.

How close are we to that moment? Perhaps very close. Certainly closer than we think.

One final word: If Jesus were to come back today, would you be ready to meet Him? If you say, "I hope so" or "I'm not sure," you aren't ready at all. If you don't know Him, you aren't ready to meet Him.

But you can become ready by opening your heart and trusting Him as your Savior and Lord. Run to the cross. Lay hold of the bleeding form of the Son of God. Rest all your hope in what Jesus Christ did when He died on the cross and rose from the dead. Rest your full weight on Jesus; pin all your hopes on Him. Lay aside your trust in anything you have done, and trust in Jesus Christ alone.

We ought to face the future with optimism. The world looks at all the problems and says, "Is there any hope?" For those who know Jesus Christ, there is enormous hope. If He comes today, we win. If He comes in fifty years, we win. If He comes in 1,000 years, we win.

GREAT DAYS TO BE ALIVE

These are great days to be alive, the greatest days in all human history. Think of it. We may well be the generation privileged to see the return of Jesus Christ. If this really is the terminal generation, the smartest thing you can do is to give your life 100 percent to Jesus Christ, so that if He comes today or tomorrow or next week or next year or in a hundred years, you will have no regrets but will be ready to see Him when he returns.

Are you ready?

SOMETHING TO THINK ABOUT

If there ever was an hour when men should consider their personal relationship to Jesus Christ, it is today. God is saying to this generation, "Prepare for the coming of the Lord."

—JOHN F. WALVOORD

QUESTIONS TO CONSIDER

1. Why has the Second Coming of Christ always been considered a fundamental Christian doctrine? What happens when this truth is denied, ignored, or minimized?

2. Name several "signs" that indicate we may be living in the last days before Christ returns to the earth.

3. Do you believe Christ will return in your own lifetime? Why or why not?

4. Why is it so important that Jesus *Himself* is coming back?

5. Think for a moment of your family and closest friends. Do

they have a relationship with Jesus Christ? What will happen to them when Christ returns?

6. Are you personally looking forward to Christ's Second Coming? Are you ready to meet Him when He comes?

SCRIPTURES TO PONDER

Acts 1:10-11
1 Corinthians 15:51-58
1 Thessalonians 4:13-18

POSTSCRIPT:
I'LL SEE YOU IN HEAVEN

As we wrap up our journey together, it occurs to me that you probably have many questions in your mind. In writing this little book, I intentionally kept the chapters short so you wouldn't lose interest. But in the process I deliberately left out a great deal of material about what Christians believe and why we believe it.

I hope this book has whetted your appetite to read more and to go deeper in the Christian faith. (See the Recommended Further Reading list later in this book.) For every chapter you could find hundreds of books discussing each topic in more depth. Some are in print; others you could locate in a good library. If my writing has stimulated you to think more seriously about your own faith, then this book has been a resounding success. Even if you don't agree with everything I've said, as long as you're wrestling with the issues, we have not wasted our time together.

Please keep reading. Solomon reminds us, "Of making many books there is no end" (Ecclesiastes 12:12). Growing Christians never stop learning because there is always more truth to discover from God's Word. The most important book you can read is the Bible itself. Don't let my book—or any other book—keep you from the pages of Holy Scripture. There you will find the ultimate truth about God, Christ, the Holy Spirit, and every other topic we have discussed. As you read, you'll find that many of your questions are answered by the Bible itself. And you'll soon discover other questions that had never occurred to you before. That's the beauty of reading the Word of God. It's like a well of cool water that never runs dry no matter how many times you drink from it. And you never reach the bottom no matter how far you lower the bucket.

I'd like to wrap up our journey together by asking you to go back to the Table of Contents and survey the chapter titles. Here's a little quiz for you. According to each chapter, what do Christians believe about the Bible, God, Jesus Christ, the Holy Spirit, and so on? What do you personally believe in each area? Your answers may be the same, or they may be quite different in some instances.

The most important question you'll ever answer is about Jesus Christ. *What do you believe about Him?* No other question matters as much as that one. In the end that question will determine your eternal destiny. What do you believe about Jesus? Have you ever trusted Him as your Lord and Savior? Becoming a Christian means trusting all that you are to all that He is. It means relying upon Him and trusting in His death and resurrection so completely that if Jesus can't take you to heaven, you aren't going there.

With this final paragraph I'm happy to tell you that I've done that. Many years ago I trusted Christ, and to this day I'm trusting Him still. If you're still unclear about Jesus and how you can know Him personally, I hope you'll go back and read the chapter on the forgiveness of sins one more time. I look forward to meeting you in heaven someday where we can sit down together and discuss these things with the One who has all the final answers.

RECOMMENDED
FURTHER READING

Those who desire to learn more about the subjects discussed in this book would find the following books especially helpful and enlightening.

E. Calvin Beisner, *Answers for Atheists, Agnostics, and Other Thoughtful Skeptics: Dialogues About Christian Faith and Life* (Wheaton, IL: Crossway Books, 1993).

Ajith Fernando, *Crucial Questions About Hell* (Wheaton, IL: Crossway Books, 1991).

Billy Graham, *Angels* (Dallas: Word, 1995).

Erwin Lutzer, *One Minute After You Die* (Chicago: Moody Press, 1997).

John MacArthur, *The Glory of Heaven* (Wheaton, IL: Crossway Books, 1996).

Josh McDowell, *Evidence That Demands a Verdict,* Volumes 1 and 2 (Nashville: Thomas Nelson, 1978, 1992).

_____. *More Than a Carpenter* (Wheaton, IL: Tyndale House, 1980).

Henrietta Mears, *What the Bible Is All About* (Glendale, CA: Regal, revised edition 1997).

Ray Pritchard, *Names of the Holy Spirit* (Chicago: Moody Press, 1995).

Joni Eareckson Tada, *Heaven: Your Real Home* (Grand Rapids, MI: Zondervan, 1995).

NOTES

CHAPTER 1

1. Andy McQuitty, "Best-seller and More," from a sermon preached at Irving Bible Church, June 18, 1995.

2. Paul Little, *Know Why You Believe* (Wheaton, IL: Victor Books, revised edition, 1987), pp. 51-52.

3. Josh McDowell and Don Stewart, *Answers to Tough Questions* (San Bernarndino, CA: Here's Life, 1980), pp. 4-6. See also the extensive discussion in Josh McDowell, *Evidence That Demands a Verdict* (San Bernarndino, CA: Here's Life, 1972), pp. 46-48.

4. McDowell, *Evidence That Demands a Verdict*, p. 175.

5. E. Schuyler English, *Ordained of the Lord* (Neptune, NJ: Loizeauax Brothers, 1976), pp. 98-101.

6. Anna B. Warner wrote this beloved children's hymn in 1860.

CHAPTER 2

1. I am grateful to Andy McQuitty, pastor of Irving Bible Church, Irving, Texas, for providing much useful material for this chapter.

2. Andrew Hermann, "91% of Chicagoans Pray, Poll Says," *Chicago Sun-Times*, September 10, 1995.

3. Anthony Campolo, *A Reasonable Faith* (Waco, TX: Word, 1983), p. 12.

CHAPTER 3

1. Much of the material in this section comes from John Stock, "The God-Man," in *The Fundamentals* (Grand Rapids, MI: Kregel, 1990), pp. 279-292.

2. This story is cited by Wilbur Smith, *Therefore Stand* (Grand Rapids, MI: Baker, 1974 reprint), pp. 586-587.

3. Cited in Josh McDowell, *Evidence That Demands a Verdict* (San Bernardino, CA: Here's Life, 1972), p. 133.

4. C. S. Lewis, *Mere Christianity* (Glasgow: Fontana, 1955), pp. 55-56. This is one of the most famous quotes of the last half-century. It shows the utter absurdity of watering down the New Testament's picture of Jesus. It

can't successfully be done without doing violence to the plain meaning of the Gospel writers.

CHAPTER 4

1. William E. Brown, *Making Sense of Your Faith* (Wheaton, IL: Victor Books, 1989), pp. 104-108.

2. D. James Kennedy, *Why I Believe* (Waco, TX: Word, 1980), pp. 148-149.

3. Robert Boyd Munger develops this image beautifully in his classic booklet *My Heart Christ's Home*, available in several versions from several publishers.

CHAPTER 5

1. Evolution refers to the belief that all life on earth has developed from nonliving matter and has progressed from simplicity to complexity over time. Tom Bethell offers a simple four-word definition: Evolution is the belief that "all organisms had parents."

2. See the discussion in Wilbur Smith, *Therefore Stand* (Grand Rapids, MI: Baker, 1974 reprint), pp. 332-341.

3. Schaeffer made that point in a little pamphlet called *No Final Conflict*, which is included in the five-volume *Collected Works of Francis Schaeffer* (Wheaton, IL: Crossway Books, 1982).

4. Ray Bohlin ("Why We Believe in Creation," Probe Ministries Internet Web Site) points out that the New Testament writers referred to Genesis 1—11 more than 100 times and that on six different occasions Jesus referred to events in the first seven chapters of Genesis. It is impossible to separate the early chapters of Genesis from the rest of the Bible.

5. Cecil F. Alexander wrote the hymn "All Things Bright and Beautiful" in 1848.

CHAPTER 6

1. Cited by Gordon Thiessen, "Lessons From a Sports Legend," *Sharing the Victory*.

2. I am grateful to Greg Bowman for loaning me his videotape of Mickey Mantle's funeral.

3. Some of these topics were provided by Andy McQuitty, in his sermon "The Great Escape," July 9, 1995, p. 1.

4. Dr. Graham gave this illustration during his sermon on March 17, 1995. I retrieved the sermon from the Christianity Online section of America Online.

5. J. R. Grider, "Forgiveness," *Evangelical Dictionary of Theology*, ed. Walter Elwell (Grand Rapids, MI: Baker, 1984), p. 421.

6. D. James Kennedy, *Why I Believe* (Waco, TX: Word, 1980), p. 189.

7. John W. Montgomery, *How Do You Know There Is a God?* (Minneapolis: Bethany, 1973), pp. 60-61.

8. Augustus M. Toplady wrote "Rock of Ages" in 1776.

CHAPTER 7

1. Cited by Brian Bill in his sermon "Angels Among Us: The Good Guys," February 12, 1995. River Valley Community Church, Rockford, Illinois.

2. *The Public Pulse*, Volume 10, Number 1.

3. *Newsweek*, November 13, 1995, p. 64.

4. Ibid., p. 65.

5. I don't mean to imply that angels and demons don't exist or that we don't encounter them in various ways in the world today. They do and we do. However, many of the reports about encounters with angels and demons include faulty and even dangerous theology. That's why we must base our thinking on God's Word and evaluate our experiences in the light of what it says.

6. For a helpful survey on angels, see Billy Graham, *Angels* (Dallas: Word, 1994). Mark Bubeck offers a great deal of helpful material on demons and demonism in *The Rise of Fallen Angels* (Chicago: Moody Press, 1995).

7. Consider the story of Elisha and his servant at Dothan in 2 Kings 6:8-17. No doubt if our eyes were opened in the same manner, we would be startled by the heavenly hosts gathered all around us.

8. Gabriel Fackre, "Angels," *Preaching*, November/December 1995, p. 4.

9. For instance, see the strong warnings in Leviticus 19:26, 28 and Deuteronomy 18:9-14.

10. This point is made very effectively by David Pawlison in his excellent book *Power Encounters* (Grand Rapids, MI: Baker, 1995), pp. 66-69. Contemporary deliverance ministry usually emphasizes that as sin gains a "foothold" in the believer's life (cf. Ephesians 4:27), it allows demons to enter and take control, creating a demonized state similar to the demon possession of the Gospels. However, nowhere does the Bible

explicitly connect demonization with personal sin. In point of fact, the Gospels are silent on *how* these unfortunate people became demonized. Many people assume that they must have followed some pattern of gross sin, but the Bible does not say that.

11. See 1 Timothy 4:1 and the Parable of the Weeds (Matthew 13:24-30, 36-43). Revelation 12:12 explicitly declares that during the Tribulation the devil will unleash his fury on the earth because he knows that his time is short.

12. For documentation, see the startling stories in Chapter 3, "Confronting Demonic Activity," in Mark Bubeck, *The Rise of Fallen Angels* (Chicago: Moody Press, 1995), pp. 55-66. Mark Bubeck's approach to this subject is biblical and pastoral; it is free from sensationalism but very frank about demonic activity in various parts of the world today.

13. This is obviously a difficult concept because it touches the larger question of why a loving God would permit evil and suffering in the perfect universe He created. However, if Satan can ever—even for one moment—do a single evil deed *in complete independence of God*, then he is in fact greater than God. And that is impossible.

CHAPTER 8

1. For a further discussion of some of these options, see Peter Kreeft and Ronald K. Tacelli, *Handbook of Christian Apologetics* (Downers Grove, IL: InterVarsity Press, 1994), pp. 227-228.

2. "The Devil Made Them Say It: Many Believe in Hell," *Chicago Tribune*, June 2, 1991.

3. Read books based on near-death experiences with great discernment. Many are filled with various unbiblical notions, and nearly all of them lean toward some form of universalism (the false view that eventually everyone will go to heaven).

4. Three times the writer of Hebrews uses a Greek word that means "to come near" or "to approach closely."

5. I mean by this that heaven includes the Old Testament saints who by faith trusted in God's Word and looked forward to God's redemption at Calvary (which they did not fully understand) and also includes every true believer from every continent and every denomination who has left this life. Everyone who has genuinely trusted in Christ as Lord and Savior will be there. I also think that young children who die go to heaven, and I would also include those born with such mental limitations that they cannot understand the Gospel.

6. William Pettingill and R. A. Torrey, *1001 Bible Questions Answered* (New York: Inspirational Press, 1997), p. 157. This is a reprint in one volume of two books first published many years ago. I highly recommend it as a handy reference tool for Bible students and Sunday school teachers.

7. W. A. Criswell and Paige Patterson, *Heaven* (Wheaton, IL: Tyndale House, 1991), pp. 33-38. He also says that in heaven we can eat all we want and not get fat. I certainly hope he's right about that.

8. Pascal's wager is explained in greater detail by Peter Kreeft and Ronald K. Tacelli in *The Handbook of Christian Apologetics* (Downers Grove, IL: InterVarsity Press, 1994), pp. 85-86.

9. D. James Kennedy, *Why I Believe* (Waco, TX: Word, 1980), pp. 69.

10. The report was given to me by Bill and Sandy Lopiccolo as part of their "Spiritual Mapping" project for a class at Trinity Evangelical School of Divinity.

11. The cartoon comes from the November 22, 1995 edition of the *Wall Street Journal*.

CHAPTER 9

1. Jeffrey Sheler, "Dark Prophecies," *U. S. News and World Report*, December 15, 1997.

2. Other doctrines could be mentioned—especially the doctrine of the Trinity. However, I believe a proper understanding of Jesus as the Son of God leads logically to the Trinity.

3. Although I believe in a Pre-Tribulation rapture of the church, I decided not to emphasize that fact in this chapter. I chose instead to look at the Second Coming as one great event with many different aspects—a view shared by most Christians.

4. See Charles R. Erdman, "The Coming of Christ," *The Fundamentals* (Grand Rapids, Kregel, 1990 reprint), pp. 695-703. Much of the material in this chapter comes from his article—originally written more than eighty years ago.

5. Although it may seem tedious to put the matter as I have, I wish to emphasize that it is Jesus Himself who is returning—not "Jesus Junior" or "Jesus II" or "Someone who looks like Jesus" or a "substitute Jesus." The same Jesus who lived and died and rose from the dead 2,000 years ago is coming again to the earth.

6. This is the same cloud of glory that overshadowed the mercy-seat in the

Holy of Holies on the Day of Atonement. It is also the same cloud that enveloped Christ on the Mount of Transfiguration (Matthew 17:5).

7. *The Biblical Illustrator* (Grand Rapids, MI: Baker, 1998 reprint), Acts, Vol. 1, pp. 73-74.

SPECIAL NOTE

If you would like to contact the author, you can reach him in the following ways:

By letter:	Ray Pritchard
	Calvary Memorial Church
	931 Lake Street
	Oak Park, IL 60301
By E-mail:	PastorRay@cmcop.org
Via the Internet:	www.cmcop.org